FOOD
UNWRAPPED

FOOD
UNWRAPPED

DANIEL TAPPER

BANTAM PRESS

LONDON • TORONTO • SYDNEY • AUCKLAND • JOHANNESBURG

TRANSWORLD PUBLISHERS
61–63 Uxbridge Road, London W5 5SA
www.transworldbooks.co.uk

Transworld is part of the Penguin Random House group of companies
whose addresses can be found at global.penguinrandomhouse.com

Penguin
Random House
UK

First published in Great Britain in 2015 by Bantam Press
an imprint of Transworld Publishers

A CIP catalogue record for this book
is available from the British Library.

ISBN 9780593073612

Typeset in 11/15.5pt Minion by Falcon Oast Graphic Art Ltd.
Printed and bound by Clays Ltd, Bungay, Suffolk

Penguin Random House is committed to a sustainable
future for our business, our readers and our planet. This book
is made from Forest Stewardship Council® certified paper.

MIX
Paper from
responsible sources
FSC® C016897

1 3 5 7 9 10 8 6 4 2

Contents

FOOD
UNWRAPPED

Introduction

Britain – once the culinary backwater of the world – has unwittingly become a nation of foodies. These days you cannot open a magazine, peruse a web page or turn on a television without being bombarded with images of succulent food, celebrity chefs or amateur competitive cook-offs.

The shelves of our supermarkets are spilling over with exotic ingredients, gastro-style ready meals and specialist foods to suit a plethora of dietary needs and fads; our cities boast a liturgy of European-style delis, specialist butchers, cafés and restaurants that would make a Parisian weep with jealousy. And British cuisine, long consigned to the culinary doldrums, is basking in glory as well-known chefs rediscover and re-invent some of the country's most iconic dishes.

Our insatiable obsession with all things food seems to be paying off. According to one recent survey, most of us now boast a hearty repertoire of around a dozen dishes we can cook without the aid of a recipe, while dishes we once agreed were best left to professionals (risottos, cheese soufflés and coq au vin, to name but a few) are being bashed out on a daily basis the nation over. Not bad for a country whose list of culinary staples once comprised Smash, Spam and Bovril.

So we know how to cook. Or at least we're a lot better at it than we once were. But how many of us actually know how our favourite foods are made? Not how they can be combined with other ingredients to make a dish, but where they originate, who invented them, how they are processed, the ways in which they affect our bodies and the science behind their flavours.

When it comes to questions like these, it could be argued that we've never known less about the food on our plate. This is hardly surprising. Thanks to the burgeoning influence of globalization, the meals we eat increasingly feature ingredients from almost every continent on earth, including countries some of us have never even heard of. And huge leaps in the arenas of science and food technology mean that even the most innocuous-looking foods can harbour hundreds of highly complex ingredients that nobody but scientists would have a hope of pronouncing – let alone understanding. If that weren't perplexing enough, we are constantly bombarded with wildly conflicting dietary advice relating to the health effects of different foods.

Food Unwrapped is all about cutting through the marketing babble and sensationalist media reports to once and for all set the record straight when it comes to the food on your plate. It's about answering those niggling questions you've always wanted to ask or have asked but have never quite got to the bottom of. But most importantly, it's about telling the amazing tale of food and the ingenious ways in which humans have spent the last several thousand years smoking, salting, stewing, brewing, brining, blending and distilling their way into the twenty-first century – giving rise to the foods we all consume today. Think champagne is a French invention? Think again. Convinced all 'artificial' foods are bad for you? Don't be so sure. Burning to find out the origin of probiotic bacteria? You might not want to know . . .

I

Is it OK for a vegetarian to drink beer?

IT'S SAFE TO SAY that Brits quite like their beer. In the UK we get through nearly six billion litres of the stuff a year. That's a staggering 93 litres per person. And despite being at the tail end of one of the worst recessions in history we still manage to cobble together an incredible £17 billion a year to spend on it (worryingly, that's more than we're prepared to expend on fruit and vegetables).

Think that's impressive? Our forefathers make us sound like teetotallers. In medieval Britain beer was drunk like water. Literally. The water in towns and cities was so polluted it was undrinkable. Therefore beer, which is sterilized during production, became not just a valuable source of nutrients but a safe source of hydration, too. According to the eminent twelfth-century historian William of Malmesbury, the English turned up for the Battle of Hastings so drunk they attacked the Normans 'more with rashness and precipitate fury than with military skill'.

Britain's love affair with all things beer refused to wane even with the enlightenment brought by the Industrial Revolution. Not content with creating the world's biggest and fastest trains, lathes and steam engines, Brits turned their technical ingenuity to brewing. Beer vats became so ambitiously massive that one particularly large vessel at London's Meux Brewery exploded in 1814, sending a tidal wave of beer through the

West End so large it destroyed entire houses and killed eight people.

Not that this dampened our appetite. Beer was so important to British morale during the Second World War that the mine-laying ship HMS *Menestheus* was converted into a floating brewery to supply beer to Allied troops. And by 1979 Britain had officially invented the binge drinker. That year over 120,000 Brits were arrested for drunkenness – more than at any other time in recorded history and four times the number of people arrested in 2012.

With such a long and, arguably, impressive history of beer swilling you'd think we'd know exactly what goes into a pint. Beer has always been made in the same way, right? You take hot water, add it to malted barley, drain away the hot sugary liquid (or 'wort'), boil it with hops and then leave it to ferment with yeast. Simple.

In reality, brewers have long been adding unusual ingredients to their beer, many of which come from animals. Honey, for example, has been used in brews since around 2000 BC and continues to be used today thanks to its high fermentability. And let's not forget cock ale, a popular tipple in eighteenth-century England made with a parboiled, skinned and gutted cock, along with various fruits and spices. In his book *Pharmacopoeia extemporanea* (1710) British physician Thomas Fuller explained that this delicious-sounding ale 'sweetens the acrimony of the blood and humours, incites clammy phlegm, facilitates expectoration, invigorates the lungs, supplies soft nourishment, and is very profitable even in consumption itself, if not too far gone'.

Tempted to give it a try? Then here's a recipe for cock ale from the *Compleat Housewife* (1727): 'Take ten gallons of ale, and a large cock, the older the better; parboil the cock, flay him, and stamp him in a stone mortar till his bones are broken; then put the cock into two quarts of sack, and put to three pounds of raisins of the sun stoned, some blades of mace, and a few cloves; put all these in a canvas bag and a little before you find the ale has done working, put the ale and bag together in a vessel; in a week or nine days time bottle it up.' Delicious.

Unusual ingredients derived from animals continued to be added to beer in recent history, mainly to enhance its flavour, texture and aroma – particularly where stout was concerned. In 1907 the Mackeson's Brewery in Kent invented milk stout by combining lactose (a sugar derived from milk) with beer, to add sweetness, body and calories. And in 1938 the Hammerton Brewery in London kicked off the trend for oyster stout by adding a handful of the molluscs to each cask to impart a faint sea-like saltiness. Both these styles of beer are still produced.

These days a new breed of craft brewers are continuing the beer industry's tradition of incorporating offbeat animal-related ingredients in their brews. Italian scientists recently discovered that hornets store grape-skin yeast in their stomachs during winter – a fungus capable of fermenting wine, bread and beer. This finding inspired New York's Birreria Brewery to create the Vespa Project: a series of beers brewed using hornet yeast. More recently, American brewery Rogue Ales released Bacon Maple Ale containing – you guessed it – bacon and maple syrup.

These, of course, are examples of eccentric beers you'd never find in your local. But what about the humble pint of British cask ale? You may be surprised to find that your favourite pint actually contains a couple of ingredients from the sea – and one of them definitely isn't vegetarian.

Thanks to modern brewing techniques we as consumers have come to expect our beer to be crystal clear. In reality, beer has a natural tendency to be cloudy. During fermentation, yeast cells and proteins, largely derived from malt, form what is called a 'colloidal suspension' – essentially a haze of very small charged particles suspended in the beer. This haze can take a long time to dissipate because an electrostatic charge known as a zeta potential (stay with me) repels one particle from the next, preventing the solid particles from settling within the liquid. The end result is that the beer looks cloudy and imparts an unpleasant yeasty flavour.

There are various solutions to the problem. The first is time. Left undisturbed, most beer will 'drop bright', meaning the yeast and proteins naturally drop out of suspension and settle on the bottom of the

Twelve Unusual Ingredients You Might Find in Mass-Produced Beer

Forget oysters and bacon . . . fancy a refreshing pint of propylene glycol alginate? Or maybe a thirst-quenching glass of tannic acid? These chemicals may not be on your bucket list but if you've ever had a pint of mass-produced beer, it's likely you've sampled both.

Propylene glycol alginate – a food-grade chemical used as a foam stabilizer to create a good solid head.

Phytoestrogen – a plant-derived variation of the female hormone oestrogen, usually a by-product of the fermentation of soya.

Gum arabic – comes from the sap of the acacia tree. Commonly used to ensure your pint has a nice creamy head but also used as a fining agent to create crystal-clear beer.

Sodium hydrosulfite – used as a preservative to extend shelf life.

Tannic acid – a light-yellow granular powder specially developed to improve the clarity of beer and to give it a longer shelf life.

Ammonium phosphate – serves as a source of nitrogen for yeast.

Potassium metabisulfite – used in the brewing industry to inhibit the growth of wild yeasts, bacteria and fungi. Also used to neutralize the chloramine that has been added to tap water at source as a disinfectant.

Tartaric acid – the principal acid in grapes. Ideal for balancing overly sweet beer and wine.

Magnesium sulfate – hoppy beers sometimes have an unpleasant soapy flavour. Magnesium sulfate eliminates such flavours and accentuates a clean hop bitterness.

Dextrin – dextrin sugars are carbohydrates that are almost tasteless, do not ferment, and subsequently remain in the finished beer enhancing the mouth-feel and perceived body.

Papayotin – papaya fruit extract used to clarify beer.

Bromelain – when beer is cooled to about zero degrees Celsius it can become cloudy; this extract, derived from the stems of pineapples, is added to some beers to prevent this from happening.

vessel. The trouble is this can take weeks – and weeks. And even then the beer is not guaranteed to be crystal clear. As a result most breweries use a combination of techniques to clear their beer.

Many commercial breweries filter the vast majority of yeast and protein from their beer once fermentation is complete and before it's packaged. They do this by mechanically forcing it through layers of filter material ranging from rough (leaving some cloudiness in the beer but making it noticeably clearer) to sterile (so fine that almost all micro-organisms are removed). Beer processed in this way is said to be 'brewery conditioned' and has the added benefit of a long shelf life.

The problem, many argue, is that filtration destroys a great deal of the unique taste and aroma of beer. It also means the beer cannot be carbonated naturally because there is no residual yeast left to convert any remaining sugars into carbon dioxide. As a result a mixture of carbon dioxide and nitrogen has to be added to make it fizzy. Real ale fans will tell you that this creates an unnaturally fizzy beer that cannot be compared to the gentle carbonation produced by the slow secondary fermentation of ale left in contact with its yeast.

So how exactly is real ale cleared? With filtration and pasteurization not an option, brewers have traditionally relied on two ingredients. The first is *Chondrus crispus* (commonly called Irish moss), a species of edible red seaweed that grows abundantly along the rocky Atlantic coasts of Europe and North America. Brewers have been drying this seaweed and adding it to their brews for well over two hundred years. The reason? The soft body of the plant consists of 50 to 60 per cent of something called carrageenan, commonly used as a thickener and stabilizer in milk products such as ice cream and processed foods. This carrageenan carries a strong negative charge, which attracts those pesky positively charged protein particles. When the protein particles converge they become heavy and drop to the bottom of the fermentation tank, leaving the beer bright and clear.

The second and most common ingredient used to clear cask-conditioned beer of yeast (as opposed to protein) is something called isinglass, a substance derived from the dried swim bladders of fish. Yes, fish. A swim bladder, for those readers who have never heard of or seen one (and why would you have?), is essentially a balloon inside a fish that allows it to control its stability and buoyancy in the water. When macerated and dissolved for several weeks in diluted food-grade acid, swim bladders form a turbid, colourless, viscous solution largely made up of a protein called collagen. This collagen comprises long, positively charged molecules that when added to beer cause the negatively charged yeast particles to clump together into a gelatinous mass. This then settles to the bottom of the cask – considerably quicker than it would naturally.

There is much speculation about when this unlikely ingredient in beer-making was first used. The most likely story is that at some point in history a resourceful fisherman used a fish's swim bladder to store his ale – akin to keeping wine in a leather flask. The acidity of the beer would have caused some of the collagen in the bladder to dissolve and clarify the beer. The observant individual might have noticed this when pouring it into a drinking vessel. Eureka!

However, the process wasn't officially documented until 1797 in an edition of the *Encyclopaedia Britannica* which suggests that it was pioneered by Frenchman Pierre Pomet, chief apothecary to King Louis XIV. By combining the isinglass with malt liquor, states the entry, Pomet found that a 'vast number of curdly masses became presently formed' which became attracted to the 'feculencies of beer' which, 'with the well known laws of gravitation', resulted in the unwanted particles combining with the isinglass and falling to the bottom of the barrel.

As for the creation of this unusual ingredient, Pomet suggests isinglass was made in the following way: 'the sinewy parts of the fish are boiled in water till all of them be dissolved that will dissolve; then the gluey liquor is strained and set to cool. Being cold, the fat is carefully taken off, and the liquor itself is boiled to a just consistency, then cut to pieces and made into a twist, bent in the form of a crescent: then hung upon a firing and carefully dried.'

Traditionally, isinglass for brewing purposes was derived from sturgeon, especially beluga sturgeon which yielded the largest bladders. These days most is obtained from tropical fish such as Nile perch from Lake Victoria, where the species was introduced in the 1950s and is now considered invasive, blamed for causing the extinction of several hundred native marine animals. The best-quality finings, however, originate in the South China Sea and are identified as Round Saigon or Long Saigon finings. The swim bladder is sun-dried at the catch site and then packed for export to markets in China, where it is used to make fish maw soup, or the UK, to make isinglass for finings.

So, is beer vegetarian? Well, it depends how strictly you define vegetarianism. Those who do take issue with isinglass can rest assured that only a trace amount of swim bladder extract ever ends up in your glass. Isinglass is so potent that for every 40 litres of ale only around half a litre is added. Most is left at the bottom of the cask along with the yeast and proteins it has attached itself to. In fact the amount is so small that breweries are not even required to list isinglass as an ingredient. Technically it's a processing aid.

If you're still not convinced, there's some good news: isinglass is now largely confined to cask-conditioned real ales, which account for only around 10 per cent of beer sales. And thanks to modern filtration technology there are hundreds of award-winning vegetarian beers to try.

A Selection of Vegan and Vegetarian Beers

If you're a strict vegetarian or vegan, you'll know how difficult it is to buy beer that's suitable for your diet. But not all beers are made with the clarifying agent isinglass. Here are some alternatives that do not contain this animal extract:

Eco-Warrior 4.5%: Essex's Pitfield Brewery has been producing organic beers for over twenty-five years. Their flagship brew, Eco-Warrior, is a vegan pale ale brewed with zingy lager hops and aromatic ale yeast. Famed among beer aficionados for its silky smooth honey flavour and gentle bittersweet, citrus finish. (pitfieldbeershop.com)

Monkman's Slaughter 6%: A multi-award-winning full-bodied bitter with a distinct malty flavour. Made by the Cropton Brewery, North Yorkshire, using exceptional pale, crystal and roasted malts combined with aromatic Kent Challenger and Goldings hops. Very strong and extremely moreish. (croptonbrewery.com)

Dubbel 8.5%: All of the beer from Manchester's Marble Brewery is manufactured using vegetarian ingredients sourced from non-intensive agriculture, including this delicious take on a traditional Belgian ale. If you like this, then you'll also love the Marble Saison made using fruity Belgian farmhouse yeast. (marblebeers.com)

Entire Stout 4.5%: This rich, sweet, velvety smooth stout from the Hop Back Brewery in Wiltshire was awarded Champion Winter Beer of Britain in 2011. Look out for its trademark aroma of caramel, chocolate and coffee. The best thing? It's 100 per cent vegan. (hopback.co.uk)

India Pale Ale, Citra 7.3%: When it comes to craft beer, nobody does it quite as well as the Kernel Brewery. All the beers from this hip London brewery are vegetarian (unless stated on the label) but their best beer is undoubtedly this fresh, citric IPA, bursting with big floral American hops. (thekernelbrewery.com)

2

How do you make my prawns so big?

PRAWNS CHANGED IN THE 1980s. Like haircuts, T-shirts and jean knee holes, they started to grow. At one time a nitpicky, pellet-sized shell concealing a thimble's worth of flesh, the humble prawn became a beast boasting an exotic new name and a sweet, meaty posterior that tasted every bit as good as lobster.

We've never looked back. *Penaeus monodon* (or the tiger prawn, as we now know it) is praised by our highest-profile chefs, found on the menus of our hippest restaurants, and is virtually up there with cod and haddock when it comes to supermarket sales. It's easy to see why. They're flavoursome, easy to cook and cheap enough to count as an affordable treat. If that isn't enough, they're healthy, too. Tiger prawns are an extremely good source of protein and very low in fat and calories. They're also a rich source of omega-3 fatty acids and vitamins E and B12.

But where do they actually come from? Tiger prawns are native to the coasts of the Indian Ocean, including South Africa, Australia and South East Asia, where they spend their lives in estuaries, lagoons and mangrove areas. If you're now imagining a lone fisherman deftly tossing his net into crystal-clear blue waters, you'd be very wrong. It's estimated that Britain alone spends a stomach-bloating £300 million on importing prawns every year. Such a glut of large warm-water prawns could never be achieved by natural harvest from the ocean.

With such a high level of demand, prawn farming has grown rapidly. In fact the tiger prawn is now one of the most widely farmed marine species in the world. It all started with the so-called Blue Revolution of the 1980s, which saw a huge and unprecedented expansion of intensive aquaculture (fish farming to you and me) in the coastal regions of Africa, Latin America and Asia. Since then global production of prawns has grown at a heady rate of 10 per cent every year, making them the world's most valuable traded marine commodity. The biggest producers today include China, India, Vietnam, Brazil, Ecuador and Bangladesh. But of all the countries involved, one is making a bigger splash than every other: Thailand.

It seems most likely that Chinese immigrants were responsible for the introduction of prawn farming to coastal Thailand in the 1930s. The method they used to catch the prawns was, in a word, genius. Low-lying coastal paddy fields were flooded during the dry season. Every time the fields were flooded, the seawater brought with it an entire supply of wild prawns. When the water retreated these prawns, and their eggs, were left stranded. If that wasn't cunning enough, the farmers didn't have to spend a bean on feeding the prawns because the tide also brought with it an abundant supply of naturally occurring marine organisms.

Prawn farming in Thailand continued like this pretty much until the 1970s when the Thai Department of Fisheries began a massive financial investment in the industry, heralding the start of a newer, more efficient way of farming. Instead of relying on the tide to bring in new stock, baby prawns were grown in hatcheries. And these weren't just any old prawns, they were tiger prawns, famed for their humongous size, which they reach in a matter of months even in artificial conditions. These prawns were then reared in high-density ponds with access to anti-biotics and protein-rich feed. The result? The number of prawns being harvested skyrocketed. This astonishingly efficient system continued to develop, and today Thailand is the biggest exporter of farmed prawns in the world, boasting a fish-farming industry like no other.

Were it not for the lack of windows, visitors to one Thai producer on the outskirts of Bangkok could be forgiven for thinking they were entering a Silicon Valley office complex. Beyond the neat landscaped gardens and sleek, chrome-clad reception is one of the world's largest prawn processing plants: a room the size of an aircraft hangar filled with the hum and whirr of over a thousand workers in face masks, latex gloves and aprons all performing the same task – de-shelling. The jumbo-sized prawns arrive in torrents, spewed from the mouth of a vast steel pipe and on to a fast-moving conveyor belt. Every worker is paid according to the number of prawns they can process per hour. And the pace is furious. With the aid of a nifty metal thumb-pick, each person gets through around seven hundred per hour. That's one prawn de-headed, de-shelled and cleaned every five seconds. Over half a million prawns are processed every day in this factory alone.

Many of the billions of prawns that pass through Thailand's processing plants every year begin their lives not in the deep blue ocean but in vast, shallow, murky ponds along the coast of the Gulf of Thailand. Some of these ponds are filled with up to two million tiger prawns, bred for their colossal size. Ensuring a constant supply of prawns of this size and quality are Thailand's commercial hatcheries, which select the very largest males and females, either from the ponds or the sea, and use them as breed stock, artificially inseminating the females.

And how on earth do you artificially inseminate a prawn? It's a highly skilled, time-consuming process involving squeezing and tweezering out sperm from live males and then rubbing the sperm over the female while she's ovulating. A moderately straightforward process were it not for the fact that the stress of captivity can limit the number of eggs the female prawns produce.

The solution for that is something called eyestalk ablation – in other words, eye removal. After mating, every live female prawn in the hatchery has one or both of her eyes pulled or sliced off. This has the effect of altering the prawn's hormones, which in turn results in ovarian development, thus stimulating the production of eggs. The larvae are then cared for in nursery tanks and transferred into the ponds once they develop into young adults. This isn't an unusual practice outlawed by the West but a normal technique used by nearly every commercial prawn hatchery in the world. Indeed the practice is accepted by the United Nations Food and Agricultural Organization (FAO) as a humane way to improve efficiency.

In the Know: Eyestalk Ablation

What: The process of eyestalk ablation (or eye removal) is used in almost every prawn reproduction facility in the world to stimulate female prawns to develop mature ovaries and spawn.
Why: Female tiger prawns do not naturally reach the later stages of ovarian maturation in captivity. Eyestalk ablation increases total egg production and the percentage of females in a given population who will participate in reproduction.
How: Eyestalk ablation is accomplished in the following ways:
1. Simply pinching and pulling off the eyestalk with the thumb and forefinger. This method may leave an open wound.
2. Slitting off one of the prawn's eyes with a razor blade, then using the thumb and index finger to squeeze out the contents of the eyestalk.
3. Cauterizing the eyestalk with red-hot wire or forceps.
4. Ligation by tying off the eyestalk tightly with surgical or other thread.

The millions of prawns produced as a result of this practice take around a hundred days of feeding to reach the size that makes them valuable on the world market; to fetch top prices they need to weigh enough to total twenty to thirty prawns per kilo. So how do they get so big? Spend a day peering through the security fence around some of

Thailand's more intensive prawn farms and you'll see men pouring buckets of a talcy acrid powder into the ponds. This stuff is known as fishmeal (or trash fish, as the industry calls it), a high-protein aquaculture feed made from ground-up fish that don't make the grade for human consumption. For years environmental groups have raised concerns about the damage done to ecosystems by the sprawling man-made ponds the prawns are reared in. Thailand's mangrove forests are among the most productive ecosystems on the planet, and act as a breeding ground for a huge variety of living creatures including fish, mammals, reptiles and migratory birds. They have important functions for humans, too. The roots of mangrove trees physically protect shore-lines from the erosive impact of waves, storms and tsunamis. They also provide a sustainable source of income for local people who use them to harvest fish and timber. On a global scale they've been shown to reduce carbon in quantities comparable to the reductions effected by rainforests, which mean they may play a role in lessening the effects of climate change. There are currently no precise figures on how great the loss of mangrove forests is, but some reports claim global mangrove deforestation now exceeds that of tropical rainforests, and nearly 40 per cent of that destruction can be attributed to prawn farming.

So how can you ensure the prawns you eat are responsibly sourced? Encouragingly, increasing pressure and criticism from environmental campaigners and consumer countries has led to stronger regulation and changes in the industry. As a result consumers now have the option to buy sustainably produced prawns. According to the Marine Conservation Society (MCS), you should always stick to buying prawns from suppliers that can ensure their product is 'responsibly farmed'. These are prawns that have been sourced from farms that comply with high environmental standards for habitat protection. Organic prawns are another option, because their producers are required to keep stocking densities down, limit the amount of chemicals they use, and recycle by-products from human-consumption fisheries for prawn feed. Those put off the idea of farmed prawns altogether (no matter how impressive their environmental credentials) can opt for sustainably caught wild prawns instead. These include cold-water prawns from the North Atlantic, caught using modified nets to reduce by-catch, and pot- or creel-caught Dublin Bay prawns from the Irish Sea, which are so delicious that most are currently exported to France.

Savvy Shopper: A Buyer's Guide to Sustainable Prawns

The species: The tiger prawn is one of the largest of the prawn and shrimp family, the *Penaeidae*. They can live up to two years in the wild, although farmed prawns are usually harvested at around six months. The tiger prawn accounts for over 40 per cent of global consumption of prawns and is the most commonly farmed marine species in South East Asia. Around 99 per cent of all tiger prawns are farmed in developing countries.

The problem: Tiger prawns are usually farmed in the tropics, sometimes very intensively and in ways that can seriously damage local communities and the environment.

The solution: Only buy tiger prawns from suppliers that can ensure their product is sourced from farms that comply with environmental standards for habitat protection and impacts of production. Going organic is often a great way to ensure this. For a more local option go for Scottish langoustines (also known as Dublin Bay prawns). Or look out for Marine Stewardship Council (MSC)-certified products.

What to Buy

Marks and Spencer: MSC cold-water prawns
Sainsbury's: Organic prawns, MSC-certified Canadian cold-water prawns and Scottish langoustines
Waitrose: Organic king prawns and MSC-certified Canadian cold-water prawns

3

What is formed ham?

B E IT OAK SMOKED, honey roast, wafer thin or shaped like a teddy bear's face, pre-sliced formed ham is a weekly staple the vast majority of us couldn't do without. UK households splurge around £1 billion a year on the stuff, most of which ends up in ham sandwiches – our most popular lunchtime snack. Yet for a country so enamoured with this meaty convenience food, most of us know surprisingly little about it – which might be a blessing when you learn how it's made.

The story of ham starts with our ancient ancestors who, prior to the advent of the supermarket and the fridge, had to dream up ingenious ways to prevent their food from spoiling, particularly in the winter when fresh food was hard to come by. These days many consider preserving food to be a luxury – something you do to impart flavour, be it through brining, pickling or smoking. Back then it was a matter of life and death. Indeed the eminent historian Maria Dembinska, writing in the late twentieth century, described the preservation of food as 'the greatest worry of primitive man'. It's easy to see why. For our forefathers, hunting animals for consumption was an extremely difficult if not life-endangering task, even for the most competent of hunters. So if you were going to put your life on the line just to eat, you certainly weren't going to let any of the meat go past its sell-by date.

One of the first ways in which our ancestors began to get round the problem, particularly in the chilly northern hemisphere, was by burying their food in the ground. It might sound counter-intuitive but burying food actually helps to prevent it from decomposing by keeping it cool and protecting it from light and oxygen. What's more, hiding your food in the ground is an extremely effective way of ensuring it doesn't get stolen.

In warmer climates drying was the preferred method of preservation. The Ancient Greek historian Herodotus wrote 2,400 years ago of the Babylonians and Egyptians drying fish in the wind and sun. Meat was also often hung in the roofs of houses – the reason, some say, it came to be smoked: by mistake over a home fire.

The best means of preservation, however, came in the form of sodium chloride. Salt is a remarkable compound and works as a preservative in a number of ways. First, it dehydrates food by drawing water out of cells via the process of osmosis, meaning any living things within the meat are killed. Second, salt is highly toxic to most microbes because of the effect of something called osmotic concentration or water pressure: in very high salt solutions many microbes rupture due to the difference in pressure between the outside and inside of the organism. Finally, salt can be toxic to the internal processes of microbes, mortally affecting their DNA. Pretty impressive stuff for something most of us sprinkle over our chips without a second thought.

Our ancient ancestors didn't know *how* this magical white substance preserved food but they certainly knew it *did* because many of the dishes we still enjoy today were born as a direct result. The Ottomans salted their beef, simultaneously creating pastrami; the British split and salted their herring, creating the much-loved kipper; and the Ancient Greeks, of course, brined their olives (anybody who has been unlucky enough to eat an olive straight from the tree will know they are utterly vile; it's a mystery how anyone imagined they might become so delicious).

Traditionally, after hogs were slaughtered the parts that couldn't be cured easily with salt, such as the brain and tenderloin, were eaten right away, while the intestines were used to encase scrap meat, giving rise to the wonderful, mighty sausage. The big cuts of meat, however, like the thighs and legs, which couldn't be eaten in a single sitting, were cured with salt, sugar and spices then left in storage to be eaten at a later date. One of the earliest recorded descriptions of curing a hog's leg with salt can be found in *De Agri Cultura* ('On Farming'), the oldest surviving work of Latin prose, written by Roman statesman Cato the Elder in 160 BC (inquisitive cooks can try Cato's recipe for themselves – see below).

Make Your Own Ham – the Roman Way

The curing of a hog's leg with salt has a long history. This recipe comes from *De Agri Cultura*, written over two thousand years ago by Cato the Elder.

'You should salt hams in the following manner, in a jar or large pot: When you have bought the hams cut off the hocks. Allow a half-modius [about 5 litres] of ground Roman salt to each ham. Spread salt on the bottom of the jar or pot; then lay a ham, with the skin facing downwards, and cover the whole with salt. Place another ham over it and cover in the same way, taking care that meat does not touch meat. Continue in the same way until all are covered. When you have arranged them all, spread salt above so that the meat shall not show, and level the whole. When they have remained five days in the salt remove them all with their own salt. Place at the bottom those which had been on top before, covering and arranging them as before. Twelve days later take them out finally, brush off all the salt, and hang them for two days in a draught. On the third day clean them thoroughly with a sponge and rub with oil. Hang them in smoke for two days, and the third day take them down, rub with a mixture of oil and vinegar, and hang in the meat-house. No moths or worms will touch them.'

Thanks, in part, to Cato's highly influential text the curing of ham continued to grow in popularity around the world and by the fifteenth century salted hog's leg had adopted the name ham, derived from the old English 'hom' or 'hamm' meaning the hollow or bend of the knee.

Remarkably, Cato's method of preserving ham has changed very little in the last two thousand years. In fact many hams, particularly artisanal European ones, are produced in almost exactly the same way, the only difference being that the length of time the pork is cured has been extended. Serrano ham, for example, can take up to two years to cure and some of the more showy Ibérico hams from southern Spain can take up to four years. The reason? We now know that the curing process doesn't just preserve meat, oh no, it alters the quality and flavour too. This is because the longer you leave meat to cure, the more moisture is lost through evaporation, thus concentrating the muscle's umami flavour (the taste associated with savoury foods like cheese, mushrooms, shellfish and ripe tomatoes – and the basis of the flavour enhancer monosodium glutomate). Long maturation has another benefit, too: the longer you leave the meat to rest, the more time its natural enzymes have to break down the connective tissue in the muscle, making it far more tender.

As for the ham we're used to in Britain, well, that is an entirely different kettle of fish. The term 'ham' here usually refers to pork that has been cured for a relatively short period of time before being cooked and thickly sliced (as opposed to being left raw with a lengthy maturation period). That's not to say we don't have our delicacies. To name but a few: there's rich and lightly smoked York ham, traditionally served with Madeira sauce; juicy honey roast Cumberland ham served straight off the bone; and arguably the most flavoursome of them all, Shropshire Black, marinated in a tangy mix of molasses and spices. But there is a catch, of course, and that's that artisan ham, be it British or European, is expensive to buy because not only is its production time-consuming and labour-intensive, it is often made with the highest-quality meat that has the largest amounts of evenly distributed fat content. For, as any butcher will tell you, fat equals flavour.

Enter formed ham, the pre-sliced, pre-packed generic-looking pink stuff most of us put between our bread. Like many foods on our supermarket shelves, it might surprise you to learn how formed ham is produced. First the meat, taken from the muscles of a pig's hind legs, is separated from the bone. Then the cuts are washed, loaded on to a conveyor belt and passed through a machine that with the help of hundreds of needles injects the meat with a special solution. This process preserves the meat and is often a vehicle for additives, though the main ingredients in this solution are salt and water.

The salt, as we already know, helps to cure the meat, but what about the water? Because the meat used in formed ham is generally quite tough, especially once cooked off the bone, the addition of water at this stage changes the texture of the meat and makes the finished product a lot juicier. It also has another important function, for the producer at least: it increases the value of the product by adding weight. Most formed ham is now around 5 per cent water, and in some cases the water content is even higher. That's a lot of extra profit.

Now for the chemicals. Three ingredients you might not be expecting in your ham are potassium nitrate, sodium nitrate and sodium nitrite. Potassium nitrate (or saltpetre as it's commonly known) is a compound used in the manufacture of gunpowder, fireworks, propellants and pretty much anything else intended to go bang. It also happens to be exceedingly good at preventing bacterial infection. Sodium nitrate and its close relative sodium nitrite are also commonly used in the production of ham for the same reason. Sodium nitrite is particularly good at inhibiting the growth of a bacteria called *Clostridium botulinum*, the daddy of all food bacteria, which can lead to something called botulism – a horrendous type of food poisoning that if not treated immediately can result in death. These nitrates and nitrites have other benefits too. They react with a protein in the meat called myoglobin, which helps to preserve the colour of the ham. So instead of turning a dull grey when cooked, it stays a vivid pink – the colour most of us have come to associate with sliced ham. They also help to accentuate the meat's flavour.

So don't go binning your ham, as the small quantities used in food production are generally considered safe. Nitrates and nitrites also occur naturally in plants. In fact most nitrates and nitrites in our diet actually come from fruit and vegetables, processed meats accounting for only around 10 per cent of our total intake.

After being injected with water, salt and various preservatives, the cuts of meat used to make formed ham are massaged – a process that doesn't look nearly as good as it sounds. All the cuts are placed into a massive steel drum resembling a giant food mixer, which churns the meat for several hours. During this process a sticky translucent protein called myosin is released from the meat. People in the trade call this 'glue'; feel it between your fingers and you'll know why.

At this stage the meat doesn't look anything like a leg of ham, it looks more like pink, meaty soup. So how do they get it into shape? Workers fish out the sloppy bits of meat from the steel drum and force them into transparent plastic bags, which, rather ingeniously, are the shape of a leg of ham (and the truth is: most of us don't question it). At this point a leaf of paper impregnated with glucose syrup and other flavourings can be inserted to impart a smoky roast honey flavour. Finally, if the ham is to be presented as a traditional cut, a layer of fat can be stuck around the edge of the mould to make it look like a whole piece of meat. Having been injected, blended and then squeezed into a plastic bag the meat is cooked, which glues all the bits together. When released from the bag, hey presto: you have yourself a cylinder of formed pork, which can then be mechanically sliced into convenient and evenly sized portions.

But what would Cato the Elder think?

Four Things You Might Find in Formed Ham

Traditional ham making involves dry-curing legs of pork by covering them with salt and then hanging them for several weeks. Formed ham, on the other hand, can be produced in just seventy-two hours using industrialized production processes. Here's a round-up of some of the ingredients commonly used:

Water: Why sell meat when you can sell water? Most formed ham is now around 5 per cent water.

Potassium nitrate (saltpetre): A chemical compound used in the manufacture of gunpowder and fireworks that's very efficient at preventing bacterial infection.

Sodium nitrate: Used to preserve, colour and flavour meat, especially formed ham. Some studies have shown that it reacts with stomach acid to produce nitrosamines, which have been linked to gastric, oesophageal and colorectal cancer, though the small quantities used in food production are generally considered safe.

Monosodium glutamate: The most universally used flavour enhancer in all meat products. Produced by the fermentation of molasses (refined sugar). In cooked ham it often comprises around 1g per 1kg of finished product.

4

What makes chewing gum so chewable, and is it safe to swallow?

IT'S A MOMENT WE'VE all experienced. You're happily chewing a wad of gum when unforeseen circumstances bring about the need for quick disposal. Whether the cause is imminent detection by a teacher, a dearth of litter bins or an unfortunately timed hiccup, you gulp down the rubbery wad whole. It's only then the voice of your mother echoes through your mind: 'Never, ever swallow chewing gum. It'll get tangled up in your bones and wrap around your heart, or at the very least sit in your stomach for all eternity.' As the minty mass descends into your digestive system, you wonder: 'What have I done?'

In Britain 28 million people (that's nearly half the population) regularly use chewing gum and most of them will avoid swallowing it at any cost. We know this because the streets and pavements are covered with the stuff. Chewing gum now accounts for 61 per cent of all street litter in the UK and the average cost of cleaning it up from a town centre is a staggering £20,000 – and this has to be carried out several times a year. In Singapore the problem is considered so serious that chewing gum is banned unless you have a prescription for it.

However, mankind's deep-seated need to gnaw on something before spitting it out isn't a new thing. Chewing gum in various forms has existed since the Neolithic period. In 2007 an archaeology student discovered a five-thousand-year-old piece of chewing gum in Finland, made from a lump of birch bark tar. Think that's impressive? The oldest piece of chewing gum ever discovered is nine thousand years old. The well-chewed blob of honey-sweetened birch tar, complete with the teeth marks of a teenage hunter-gatherer, was found in Sweden alongside an axe and the bones of a beluga whale. Teenagers, eh?

Forms of chewing gum were also used in Ancient Greece. The Greeks enjoyed gum made from the resin of the mastic tree (the word 'mastic' is derived from the Greek verb μαστιχειν, which means to 'gnash teeth'). Originally a liquid, mastic is sun-dried into drops of hard, brittle, translucent resin. When chewed, the resin softens and becomes a bright white gum with a refreshing, slightly piney or cedar-like flavour. In Ancient Greece mastic was given as a remedy for snake bites, and in India and Persia it was used to fill dental cavities. Hippocrates of Cos, the so-called 'Father of Medicine', wrote that it was good for the prevention of digestive problems and colds; the physician Claudius Galenus suggested that it was useful for treating bronchitis and for improving the condition of the blood. In medieval times mastic was highly valued by sultans' harems as a breath freshener and tooth whitener. It has now been proved that mastic contains antioxidants and has antibacterial and antifungal properties. In fact a recently published Nottingham University study claims that it can cure peptic ulcers by killing the *Helicobacter pylori* bacteria.

The type of chewing gum favoured by Native North Americans was spruce tree resin, which they later introduced to the early pioneers. In the mid-1800s American inventor and businessman John B. Curtis became the first man to start making and selling spruce chewing gum commercially, under the name the State of Maine Pure Spruce Gum (unfortunately for Curtis the gum never really took off owing to its highly unusual flavour). In South America, the Aztecs chewed on something far tastier called chicle (pronounced 'chick-lay'), a natural gum produced from the sap of the sapodilla tree – a slow-growing evergreen species native to Central America and the Caribbean. The tapping of the gum is still carried out in the same way today. A worker, called a chiclero, climbs to the top of the tree (they can be up to 50 feet tall) and on his descent makes a series of zigzag cuts down its length, which releases a sticky white sap. The dripping sap flows down the tree and is collected at the bottom in bags before being boiled, poured into rectangular moulds and shipped off to chewing gum manufacturers.

A big fan of chewing chicle sap was Mexican politician, general and eleven-time president Antonio López de Santa Anna. In 1866 Santa Anna sent a sample of chicle to his friend and former secretary Thomas Adams, a New York businessman, scientist and inventor. Adams quickly saw the potential of chicle and immediately began experimenting with the newfangled rubbery substance. At first he used it to make toys, masks and wellington boots but none was a commercial hit. Then in 1869 he had a brainstorm: why not use the chicle as the Aztecs did but with a small amount of added sugar and flavour? Adams thus created the world's first modern chewing gum.

Success was instantaneous. By 1890 Adam's six-storey factory employed 250 workers and he had spawned a national craze. Gum chewing swept the country, and like most things that are even remotely pleasurable was soon condemned as evil by politicians and clergymen. Things got so bad that in 1890 the *New York Sun* ran an article lampooning those who chose to chew: 'The habit has reached such a stage now that makes it impossible for a New Yorker to go to the theatre or the church, or enter street cars or the railway train, or walk on a fashionable promenade without meeting the men and women whose jaws are working with the activity of the gum-chewing victim. And the spectacle is maintained in the face of frequent reminders that gum-chewing, especially in public, is an essentially vulgar indulgence that not only shows bad breeding, but spoils a countenance and detracts from the dignity of those who practice the habit.' Adams had the last laugh, however. He eventually joined The Wrigley Company, now one of the world's biggest chewing gum manufacturers, which continued to use chicle right up until the 1950s. And retired an incredibly rich man.

Some small-scale manufacturers, like British natural chewing gum company Peppersmith, still use chicle sustainably sourced from the rainforests of Central America. It's a surprisingly straightforward process. The chicle is cooked at 116°C until melted into a thick syrup, which helps to purify it, before being left in a room to dry for a day or two. The gum is then sterilized and melted in a steam cooker and pumped to a high-power centrifuge to rid the gum of any undesirable impurities like dirt or bark. Next, the gum is cooked and mixed with natural flavourings and sweeteners like xylitol (harvested from the bark of Finnish birch trees) then rolled, cooled and gently kneaded until rubbery and smooth. Finally, large chunks are chopped off, flattened by rollers and scored into a pattern of tablet-sized pieces. Small-scale factories like Peppersmith churn out around two hundred thousand pieces of chewing gum a day in this way. It might sound like a lot to get your teeth around but in comparison to some of the larger-scale chewing

Number Cruncher: Chewing Gum

$20 billion – total value of the chewing gum industry
3.74 trillion – total number of pieces of chewing gum made every year
35 – percentage of all chewing gum manufactured by Wrigley
115 – total number of chewing gum manufacturing companies
100,000 tons – amount of chewing gum consumed every year
23 inches – diameter of the largest bubblegum bubble ever blown
11 – number of calories burned after chewing gum for an hour
9,000 – the age of the world's oldest piece of chewing gum
300 – the average number of pieces of gum each person chews every year
61 – percentage of UK street litter that chewing gum accounts for
28 million – the number of Brits who regularly chew gum

gum producers it's small change. The problem with natural chewing gum is that it has to be made in small batches because chicle sap is expensive and in short supply. A sapodilla tree typically yields only 1kg of chicle every three to four years.

These days the worldwide chewing gum industry is worth a staggering $20 billion and is dominated by two extremely powerful companies, Wrigley and Cadbury, who account for over 60 per cent of worldwide production. These companies rely on a cheaper, more readily available ingredient produced by the petrochemical industry called butyl rubber (also known as polyisobutylene or PIB). This synthetic food-grade rubber produced from the polymerization (chemical bonding) of isoprene (a common organic compound) and isobutylene (a hydrocarbon derived from petroleum) was first developed in 1937 by the Standard Oil Company, which later became Exxon.

The first commercial application of PIB was in tyre inner tubes but these days you'll find it in pretty much anything requiring airtight rubber – washing-up gloves, clingfilm, rugby balls and racing tyres to name but a few. It has a number of other less conventional uses too, including being used to clean up waterborne oil spillages. When added to crude oil PIB increases the oil's elasticity, causing the oil to resist break-up when vacuumed from the surface of the water. PIB was first used to make chewing gum in the 1950s because it was found to maintain the perfect amount of chewiness even after considerable munching. The PIB used in the manufacture of chewing gum starts life as a gas but is transformed with the help of a catalyst into an extremely hot (150°C) colourless, odourless, sticky, transparent gel which can then be combined with colourings and flavourings to make chewing gum – much in the same way chicle is used.

The good news about PIB and chicle is that they're both non-toxic. But are they safe to swallow? Globally we get through around 100,000 tons of chewing gum every year (that's about 3.74 trillion pieces), and of this amount it's estimated we swallow around 30 per cent. If the legend that chewing gum stays in your stomach for seven years were true, gastroenterologists would be seeing a lot more evidence of it in endoscopies and colonoscopies.

So what does happen to chewing gum once swallowed? The truth is, not much. Pop a piece of chewing gum into your mouth and your saliva will make a valiant but ultimately useless attempt to break it down. It might penetrate some of the less hardy components such as the shell and sweeteners but the gum base will be left intact. It's then down to your stomach muscles which contract and relax, much in the way an earthworm moves, to slowly force the gum through your digestive system. It might take a couple of days but the chewing gum will eventually emerge at the other end completely intact (albeit a little worse for wear).

Nevertheless, the usually safe passage of gum through the system doesn't mean it is wise to habitually swallow it. Something called a bezoar (a rather ominous-sounding term that essentially means a large mass of indigestible matter) can form in the stomach when food or other foreign objects stick to gum and build up, causing intestinal blockage. Children, who have a smaller-diameter digestive tract than adults, are particularly susceptible. In 1998 a four-year-old boy in Britain was referred to hospital with a two-year history of constipation. The ill-fated lad was found to have 'always swallowed his gum after chewing five to seven pieces each day', having been given the gum as a reward for good behaviour. The build-up resulted in a solid mass that, quite understandably, refused to leave the boy's body. In the same year an eighteen-month-old girl required medical attention when she swallowed chewing gum and four coins, which got stuck together in the oesophagus.

It's not all bad news though. In fact chewing gum may have some considerable health benefits. Some ear, nose and throat surgeons recommend chewing gum because it encourages the production of saliva, which acts as an antibiotic to protect you from the common cold and other germs. The stimulation of extra saliva can also help to prevent tooth decay and bad breath by removing food particles and bacteria from your mouth. What's more, scientists at Cardiff University have found that chewing gum can aid concentration as well as boost mental performance, alertness and cognitive reasoning, often more than caffeine. Finally – though this one might be scraping the barrel – chewing gum for sixty minutes burns around eleven calories. Every little helps, right?

Chewing Gum and Health: the Good, the Bad and the Ugly

Chewing gum jumped from the confectionery into the well-being category just a few years ago by boasting health benefits from cavity prevention to weight control. Well, here's the news, and it's not all good . . .

The Good

Brainpower: Some scientific evidence suggests that chewing gum can boost alertness and increase reaction times by up to 10 per cent. Japanese research published in the journal *Brain and Cognition* suggests as many as eight areas of the brain are affected by the simple act of chewing. One theory to explain the improved performance is that chewing increases arousal and leads to temporary improvements in blood flow to the brain.

Oral health: According to the American Dental Association, there are a multitude of benefits associated with stimulating salivary flow through chewing, including teeth cleaning, plaque reduction, enamel strengthening and decay prevention. Additional saliva can also help to reduce the chance of gingivitis and gum bleeding. Chewing on wax would have the same effect, but who wants to do that?

(Continued)

The Bad

Bad-mouth: Chewing gum can cause mouth disorders in certain people, such as a clicking or popping noise in the jaw, or tire out jaw muscles. If a person has a pre-existing jaw condition (such as a temporomandibular joint (TMJ) disorder), chewing gum can aggravate the condition, as well as lead to extra wear and tear on the cartilage surrounding the jaw joints.

Bittersweet: Chewing gum that doesn't use helpful additives (like xylitol and calcium lactate) can be damaging for teeth. The most common ingredient in standard gums is sugar – or sweetener in sugar-free gums. Sugar has been linked with causing numerous chronic dietary problems and, of course, good old cavities.

The Ugly

If you habitually swallow chewing gum and suffer from chronic constipation then you could be host to a bezoar, a large mass that is causing a blockage somewhere in your digestive system.

5

Can a chilli physically burn you?

IN 2011 AN INDIAN restaurant in Edinburgh held a competition to eat the extra hot 'Kismot Killer Curry'. According to reports, the chillies used in the dish were so potent that by the end of the event over half of the twenty competitors had either vomited, collapsed or were writhing around in agony. One of them, an American exchange student named Curie Kim (I kid you not), was in such severe pain she was rushed to hospital by ambulance. 'It was like I was being chainsawed in the stomach,' she said. Further south, chefs at the Atomic Burger diner in Bristol have created a burger so hot it must be eaten wearing protective gloves, and only by over-eighteens who are obliged to sign a disclaimer. Those who can finish the fiery burger – made using two of the world's hottest chillies, the Bhut Jolokia and the Scotch Bonnet – have their names mounted on the restaurant's 'Wall of Flame'. Only one in ten succeeds.

In competitions that match humans against some of the world's hottest chillies there are rarely any winners. Why then do people seem to derive so much pleasure from attempting to eat something that can potentially cause so much pain? Unsurprisingly, very few living things apart from humans enjoy the burn chillies provide. In fact one of the reasons chillies have managed to thrive is because most animals (unlike those foolhardy contestants) avoid them like the plague. In 2001 a team from the University of Montana observed that, when given the choice, wild rodents almost always shunned spicy chillies in favour of other

The Scoville Guide to Chillies

The Scoville scale is a measurement of the heat of chillies, indicating how much capsaicin (the substance that makes chillies taste hot) is present. The scale is named after its creator, American chemist Wilbur Scoville, who developed the Scoville Organoleptic Test back in 1912. In his method, a solution of pepper extract is diluted in sugar syrup until the heat is no longer detectable to a panel of (usually five) tasters; the degree of dilution gives its measure on the Scoville scale. Thus a sweet pepper or a bell pepper, containing no capsaicin at all, has a Scoville rating of 0, meaning no heat detectable. Conversely, the hottest chillies have a rating of 100,000 or more, indicating that their extract has to be diluted 100,000-fold before the capsaicin present is undetectable.

Scoville rating	Type of chilli pepper
15,000,000–16,000,000	Pure capsaicin
2,000,000–5,300,000	Standard US grade pepper spray, Carolina Reaper, Trinidad Moruga Scorpion
855,000–1,463,700	Naga Viper, Infinity, Bhut Jolokia, Trinidad Scorpion Butch T
350,000–580,000	Red Savina Habanero
100,000–350,000	Habanero, Scotch Bonnet, Rocoto, Madame Jeanette, Peruvian White Habanero
50,000–100,000	Byadi, Malagueta, Bird's Eye, Piri Piri, Pequin
30,000–50,000	Gunter, Cayenne, Tabasco
10,000–23,000	Serrano, Aleppo
3,500–8,000	Espelette, Jalapeño, Chipotle

(Continued)

1,000–2,500	Anaheim, Poblano, Rocotillo, Peppadew
100–900	Pimento, Peperoncini, Banana Pepper
0	Bell Pepper, Cubanelle, Aji Dulce

food. In fact the only animals that would always opt for chillies were birds. The reason? Birds, it transpires, are completely immune to the heat of chillies. The same researchers also noted that the seeds of a chilli pass through a bird's digestive system quickly and unharmed, whereas in mice, rats and other mammals the seeds are ruined by chewing and acidic digestive juices. The burning taste of chillies, scientists suggest, is actually an evolutionary ploy to stop mammals eating and therefore destroying chilli seeds. Birds, on the other hand, are actively attracted to the bright colours of chillies and go on to disperse their seeds far and wide in their droppings.

A cunning trick performed by chillies, but if birds eat them and mammals don't, why do humans enjoy them? Chilli peppers have been enjoyed for a long time by humans and were perhaps the first plants to be domesticated in Central America; there is evidence they were consumed as far back as 7500 BC. The rest of the world didn't catch on to chillies until the sixteenth century when Christopher Columbus encountered them and brought them back to Europe. They were then introduced to India by Portuguese and Spanish explorers where they were readily incorporated into local cuisines, perhaps because people were already familiar with pungent, spicy flavours (the vindaloo is in fact a version of a traditional Portuguese dish). Exactly how the plant spread from South Asia to China and South East Asia is largely unknown, but it is assumed that local, Arab and European traders transported chillies via traditional trading routes along great waterways such as the Ganges.

One theory for the global success of chillies is that people may have initially used them as a preservative. Spices are anti-microbial: of the thirty most commonly used varieties at least half of them kill or inhibit 75 per cent of the bacteria they have been tested on. This might explain why the use of spices in meat-based recipes is most widespread in hot climates, where the growth rates of micro-organisms are highest. Other studies have attempted to explain man's love of hot food through the prism of geography. Traditionally, people living in tropical regions prefer their food hotter than those living in temperate areas. This pattern gives rise to the theory that consuming spicy food helps to combat the effects of a warm climate by making the eater sweat more, thus allowing the body to cool down.

Another, more intriguing theory, suggested by professor of psychology Dr Paul Rozin, is masochism: we are in it for the pain. He tested chilli eaters by gradually increasing the spiciness of their food right up to the point at which the subjects said they could go no further. When asked after the test what level of heat they liked the best, the subjects always chose the highest amount they could stand, just below the level of unbearable pain. Humans, Dr Rozin concluded, actively seek out sensations that are painful or scary but safe; we enjoy eating hot chillies in the same way we enjoy the sensation of falling provided by a rollercoaster, the feelings of fear and anxiety while watching horror films, or the sadness that comes with a tear-jerker. Essentially, chillies are like an edible skydive.

But can something that makes you feel like you're being 'chainsawed in the stomach' be safe? The good news about the active component in all hot chillies, capsaicin (pronounced 'cap-say-sin'), is that it doesn't actually cause any tissue damage, it merely tricks you into thinking your body is on fire. Here's how. When you eat or touch a chilli, capsaicin particles penetrate your skin and your tissue, triggering your nervous system. (It gets a bit technical now.) Capsaicin acts like a neurotransmitter and binds to nerve endings called TRPV1 receptors, forcing them to deform. Usually these receptors only deform at temperatures of

The Hottest Chillies in the World

Carolina Reaper: A hybrid chilli pepper created by cultivator Ed Currie and his company PuckerButt Pepper Company in Rock Hill, South Carolina. On 14 November 2013 the Carolina Reaper was officially named the world's hottest chilli by Guinness World Records, with individual peppers rating over 2.2 million Scoville Heat Units (SHUs).

Trinidad Moruga Scorpion: On 13 February 2012 the New Mexico State University's Chilli Pepper Institute identified the Trinidad Moruga Scorpion as the hottest chilli in the world with a heat of more than two million SHUs.

Trinidad Scorpion Butch T: Named after Butch Taylor, the owner of Zydeco Farms in Mississippi, who was responsible for propagating the chilli's seeds. So-called because the pointed end of the pepper is said to resemble a scorpion's stinger. Set the record for the world's hottest chilli back in 2011 with 1,463,700 SHUs.

Trinidad/Naga Viper: Created by English chilli farmer Gerald Fowler of The Chilli Pepper Company, based in Cark, Cumbria. At 1,382,118 SHUs it was previously the official holder of the Guinness 'World's Hottest Chilli' record as of 25 February 2011.

Bhut Jolokia: Also known as the Ghost chilli, the Bih Jolokia, the Serpent chilli, the Naga Jolokia or Naga Morich. Whatever you want to call this capsicum, it's got a reputation to precede it. At a whopping 1,041,427 SHUs it's nearly thirty times hotter than a tabasco chilli and two hundred times hotter than a jalapeño.

or above 42°C. As a result they transmit signals to the brain, the same kind we would receive if we were sensing high levels of heat. The brain is unable to detect the difference, so you experience the same pain from chilli peppers as you would from a burn. The brain responds to the burning sensation by raising your heart rate, increasing perspiration and releasing endorphins (just as it does during exercise, excitement and orgasm). This latter effect might explain why 'chilli heads' become so addicted to eating spicy food.

Human skin is relatively resistant to the effects of chilli because it's protected by a thick layer of dead skin cells, which makes it difficult for the capsaicin to reach your vulnerable nerve endings. However, at sites where the skin has a greater concentration of receptor cells, such as your eyes, mouth, nose and underneath your fingernails, there is a much higher chance of feeling the burn. When you eat a vindaloo, for example, you experience the burn as the capsaicin binds to the receptors in your mouth; the rest of the gastrointestinal tract (oesophagus to rectum) has very few TRPV1 receptors, so you do not experience the same sensation as the curry makes its way through your body. The bad news, for the morning after your vindaloo, is that capsaicin is not completely broken down by digestion and the lining of the anus is furnished with a large number of receptors. Mercifully, the effect is usually mitigated by the fact that the material in question often spends very little time in contact with your behind – unless you're particularly unlucky.

Rump burn aside, chillies can actually be good for us. It might sound counter-intuitive but chillies have been used as a form of pain relief for centuries. Native Americans rubbed their gums with pepper pods to relieve toothache (as a curiosity, they also used hot pepper extract as an aphrodisiac – a practice adopted by early settlers, to the dismay of their priests). Indeed the pain-relieving effects of chilli were believed to be so impressive that until the 1800s eunuchs serving Chinese emperors were castrated only after their scrotums had been repeatedly rubbed with hot chilli extract. More recently, scientists have begun to develop painkillers using chillies, or more specifically capsaicin, which combat the chronic pain of diseases like osteoarthritis and rheumatoid arthritis without any of the numbness associated with normal anaesthetics.

But if chillies are beneficial to our health and their burn is basically a figment of our imagination, then what about those hapless hot-curry-eating competitors in Edinburgh? It doesn't sound like Curie Kim was imagining her pain. Well, chillies might not be able to physically burn you but their effects, especially when consumed in high doses, are not to be scoffed at. Capsaicin is an irritant and when applied to the eyes or airways it can be disabling to the extent that it is used as a non-lethal weapon: pepper spray, according to the European Parliament Scientific and Technological Options Assessment (STOA), causes 'temporary blindness (lasting anywhere between 15–30 minutes), a burning sensation on the skin (which can last between 45–60 minutes), upper body spasms and uncontrollable coughing making it difficult to breathe or speak (for around 3 to 15 minutes)'. In fact capsaicin can be so effective that chilli grenades have even been developed by India's Defence Research and Development Organization and used on protesters in Kashmir.

Just as excruciating are the effects high doses of capsaicin can have on the digestive tract. The stomach's natural response to any gastro-intestinal irritation (be it too much alcohol or capsaicin) is painful stomach cramps and regurgitation, which might help to explain the effects of the 'Kismot Killer Curry'. Chillies can kill, too – theoretically. A research study in 1980 calculated that 13g of the hottest chillies in the world – something like Bhut Jolokia – eaten all at once would cause enough stomach and intestinal tissue inflammation to kill a 150lb person. However, your body would most probably reject the offending chilli before it had the chance to kill you.

Let's face it, the vast majority of readers won't be experiencing the effects of a chilli grenade any time soon; but what to do in the event of somebody slipping a Bhut Jolokia into your next curry? Fortunately there are several techniques for reducing the pain of hot chillies, and most of them involve the kind of things you'd find in your kitchen.

Firstly, under no circumstances drink water. Capsaicin is an oil, meaning it is not water-soluble. Reach for a pint of water and you will only enhance the burning sensation by spreading the capsaicin throughout your mouth. Milk and yoghurt are far better at countering the effects of chillies because capsaicin dissolves better in fatty substances. Alternatively, some people find that drinking tomato juice or biting into a lemon or lime helps to reduce the pain: their high acid content helps to neutralize the alkaline capsaicin. Better still, exercise some moderation. If the chilli you're eating is hurting too much or making you nauseous then your body is probably trying to tell you something.

How to Quell the Fire

Your eyes are watering, your nose is running, and your mouth feels like an inferno. So what do you do? Remember, don't reach for the nearest glass of water or beer: capsaicin is hydrophobic, meaning it doesn't dissolve in water. It does, however, in fats and oils, which explains why full-cream milk is the traditional choice for quelling the fire in India. 'Something with a lot of fat in it, like yoghurt or milk, is going to dissolve the compound and wash it away,' explains Mark Peacock, a plant scientist from the University of Sydney, who helped to cultivate one of the world's hottest chillies, the Trinidad Scorpion Butch T. 'My favourite remedy is olive oil,' he adds, 'but it's not the most pleasant.'

6

How do you stop coffee from giving you the jitters?

LEGEND HAS IT THAT a ninth-century Ethiopian goat herder called Kaldi discovered coffee. Noticing that when his flock nibbled on the bright red berries of a certain bush they became a little crazy and began to dance, the observant shepherd chewed on the fruit himself. Exhilarated by the effect the fruit had on him, Kaldi promptly took the berries to an Islamic monk in a nearby monastery (as you would). But the monk, disapproving of their use, threw them into a fire, from which a rich, enticing aroma billowed. Realizing his error, the monk swiftly retrieved the now roasted berries from the embers, ground them up and dissolved them in hot water – thus making the world's first cup of coffee.

Over a thousand years later and it isn't Kaldi's goats that are dancing, it's us. Coffee is now the most popular drink in the world, with around two billion cups consumed every single day; the UK alone accounts for 70 million of these. And after crude oil, coffee is the world's most traded commodity, putting it ahead of natural gas, gold, sugar and corn. When the financial crisis hit in 2007/08 coffee seemed like the first thing we would sacrifice, an unnecessary little luxury that could be dropped to save a few pennies. But even one of the worst recessions in history couldn't diminish our insatiable demand for it. The coffee-shop industry has grown at an unprecedented rate in recent years. Since 1997 the number of cafés in the UK has grown tenfold to 15,000 and that is expected to rise to 20,000 over the next four years. If we continue to buy coffee at the rate we currently do, the average Briton will spend nearly £16,000 on takeout coffees over the course of a lifetime; for the one in ten who needs an extra shot of espresso in their latte, the figure is nearer £30,000.

So what is the magic ingredient in coffee that helped it to become the non-negotiable luxury of our generation? The answer is caffeine, the world's most widely consumed psychoactive drug. In its natural state caffeine is a slightly bitter, white crystalline stimulant found in varying quantities in the seeds, leaves and fruit of some plants, where it acts as a natural pesticide that paralyses and kills certain insects. It has another important function, too: enhancing the memory of pollinators. Scientists have found that consuming naturally caffeine-laced nectar helps bees to improve their long-term memories, meaning they are more likely to return to plants of the same type. In other words, caffeine gives bees a buzz (sorry, it was hard to resist).

The Science Behind the Buzz

Caffeine – 1,3,7-trimethylxanthine, to give it its chemical name – is a member of a group of naturally occurring substances called methylxanthines. These compounds are similar in structure to adenosines, naturally occurring molecules in our bodies that aid the onset of sleep. Adenosines bond to receptor cells in the brain to calm the activity of the central nervous system, thus triggering tiredness. Caffeine molecules bind to these receptor cells but have no active effect on the nervous system. However, by doing so they take the place of adenosine molecules that could make a difference. This process is known as 'competitive inhibition' and effectively delays the onset of fatigue, increases alertness and improves people's ability to sustain attention.

In humans, caffeine acts as a central nervous system stimulant, temporarily warding off drowsiness, restoring alertness, aiding concentration and, according to some studies, improving athletic performance.

Caffeine, like any drug, doesn't come without its downsides. As anybody who has experienced a bout of the 'jitters' will testify, too much coffee equals shaky hands, insomnia and headaches. It can even cause hallucinations. Researchers at Durham University found that 'high caffeine users' – those who consumed more than the equivalent of seven cups of instant coffee a day – were three times more likely to have heard a person's voice when there was nobody there compared with 'low caffeine users' who consumed less than the equivalent of one cup of instant coffee a day. Seeing things that were not there, hearing voices and sensing the presence of dead people were among the experiences reported by some of the participants. The explanation could be that caffeine has been found to exacerbate the effects of stress, and when under stress the body releases a hormone called cortisol, which in turn can trigger hallucinatory experiences.

Caffeine can even be toxic in large enough doses. Indulge in too much and you may well experience restlessness, nervousness, abnormal heart rhythms, vomiting and, theoretically, death. What dose of caffeine is mortal is dependent on an individual's weight and sensitivity, but for the average person it is about 90mg per two pints of blood. In the real world that's about two hundred cups of instant coffee in a single day. Death would come in the form of ventricular fibrillation – an uncoordinated contraction of heart muscles which could stop blood from being pumped around the body. It should be noted here that the sheer volume of water consumed while drinking that amount of coffee would probably kill you before the caffeine did. You would effectively drown in coffee first.

So, the likelihood of somebody drinking enough coffee to kill themself is extremely low. In fact there are no recorded cases of death as a direct result of drinking too much coffee. However, caffeine, even in relatively small amounts, can make you seriously ill, especially if you're not used to it. In 2007 a seventeen-year-old girl in County Durham was taken to hospital suffering from hyperventilation and heart palpitations after consuming seven double espressos while working at her family's sandwich shop. The unfortunate teen told reporters she first knew something was wrong when she began to manically laugh and cry for no apparent reason in front of customers. Doctors confirmed she had overdosed on caffeine. If the girl had continued to drink seven double espressos a day she may well have developed caffeinism, an addiction thought to occur if you have an intake above 600mg of caffeine per day. That's roughly five to six cups of ground coffee or eight to ten cups of instant. In such cases withdrawal can be a nasty affair, resulting in headaches, irritability, depression and fatigue. Caffeine addiction isn't a new thing. In the mid-eighteenth century Johann Sebastian Bach wrote a comic opera called the *Coffee Cantata* about the perils of coffee dependence. The piece was a terrific hit when it was first performed – in, of course, a coffee house.

The negative effects of caffeine have fuelled the market for decaffeinated coffee, which is now worth an impressive $2 billion and accounts for up to 15 per cent of all the coffee we drink. But how is the caffeine removed? To qualify as decaf, coffee must be at least 97 per cent caffeine-free. The oldest way of achieving this is by using an industrial solvent called methylene chloride (MC), a highly toxic, volatile liquid with a propensity for causing cancer of the lungs, liver and pancreas among lab animals (one of the reasons the EU has banned its use in hairspray and paint stripper). The method is pretty straightforward. First, the green (unroasted) beans are steamed, which causes them to swell, opening up their pores. They are then left to sit in MC for up to fourteen hours during which time the solvent dissolves the beans' waxy coating and extracts the caffeine. Once the solvent has been drained off, the beans are rinsed with water and sent away to be roasted. Here's the clever bit: the solution containing the extracted caffeine is distilled until the solvent evaporates, leaving behind pure caffeine. This is then sold to

In the Know: Caffeine Addiction

Can't function until your morning cup of coffee? Find yourself feeling ill if you miss your daily fix? Then you could be suffering from caffeinism.

Definition: Caffeinism is a recognized mental disorder characterized by a set of behavioural and physiological symptoms caused by excessive consumption of caffeine. Symptoms can include nervousness, muscle twitching, insomnia, hallucinations, heart palpitations, gastrointestinal disturbances and an abnormally rapid rate of breathing. A daily intake of over 600mg of caffeine (roughly five to six cups of brewed coffee or eight to ten cups of instant) is too much.

Withdrawal symptoms: Like many drugs, caffeine is chemically addictive and can lead to some pretty nasty withdrawal symptoms, including headaches, tiredness, decreased energy, drowsiness, nausea, depression and irritability. The onset of symptoms typically begins twelve to twenty-four hours after withdrawal and can last for up to nine days. Not surprising, then, that people find it hard to break the habit.

Treatment: Quitting caffeine isn't easy, but if you feel your consumption has become a bad habit, the best way to break it is to create a new one in its place. Try replacing coffee with decaf coffee, herbal tea or dandelion root coffee, which tastes like coffee (sort of) but is caffeine-free and high in antioxidants.

food producers for use in a plethora of products including soft drinks, cheap chocolate, ice cream, weight-loss pills, pain relievers and energy drinks. Remarkably, this extracted caffeine is worth £20 a kilo, making it more valuable pound for pound than the coffee itself.

Sounds like a win-win situation: caffeine-sensitive consumers get to buy their lattes without fear of the jitters, while coffee processers make a mint from selling off surplus caffeine. But what about the methylene chloride – sounds like pretty scary stuff, right? Not according to the EU. They argue that MC is safe in amounts of 3ppm (parts per million) and in most decaf coffee tests it comes in at less than 1ppm. What's more, the boiling point of MC is 40°C and coffee is roasted at 190–218°C, meaning any remaining solvent should – theoretically – be well and truly vaporized before it reaches your cup.

The biggest criticism levelled at decaf, however, isn't its effect on health but on the coffee-drinking experience. Ever since German coffee merchant Ludwig Roselius developed the first decaffeination process in 1903, decaf has been the subject of scorn among coffee aficionados. Decaf coffee, many baristas will tell you, is tantamount to smoking a cigarette without nicotine – there simply isn't any point. As for flavour, many say it doesn't even come close to the real thing. There is a good reason why. Though there are several methods to remove caffeine, they all begin the same way, with soaking in water or steaming, which means the raw beans arrive in the roastery in a kind of pre-brewed state, their flavour already compromised. And in some cases there is the small matter of the MC. Though this solvent is highly adept at removing caffeine it also removes some of the four hundred other compounds that are integral to the taste and aroma of the final drink.

If drinking coffee made using a toxic solvent doesn't really do it for you, there is another way. The use of water as a solvent to decaffeinate coffee was originally developed in Switzerland in the 1980s and is now used commercially under the trademark 'Swiss Water Process'. To prepare to decaffeinate coffee using this method a solution is created by soaking a high quantity of beans in water until all the soluble components, including caffeine, seep out. The spent beans are then discarded and the fluid is passed through carbon filters that extract the caffeine. The resulting fluid is saturated with water-soluble solids (i.e. all the flavour) minus the caffeine. Now for the actual decaffeination. Fresh green beans (with caffeine) are left to soak in this concentrated flavourful fluid for eight to ten hours, during which time the caffeine migrates from the green beans into the solution as it attempts to reach equilibrium – while the other components inside the coffee stay put. Proponents claim the result is relatively flavoursome, chemical-free decaf coffee. Unfortunately the process is energy-intensive, making the decaffeinated coffee more expensive to buy than regular beans.

So what's the answer? Enter Decaffito, a strain of coffee discovered in 2004 by Brazil's Campinas Agronomic Institute that is almost completely caffeine-free. It has since been repeatedly crossbred to create a naturally caffeine-free coffee plant with the potential for large-scale cultivation. If the project succeeds it could revolutionize the decaf industry for ever because the beans are cheap to produce, safe to consume and retain the natural flavour of normal coffee. The bad news is these plants won't be available commercially for several years. Until then the choice is up to you: embrace the process or do like Kaldi's goats did and get down with the jitters.

Caffeine: Highs and Lows

Caffeine is readily absorbed into your bloodstream, processed by your liver and remains active for around five to six hours. How caffeine affects us all depends on individual tolerance but according to the *Journal of Food Science*, consuming less than 400 to 450 milligrams of caffeine per day is generally regarded as safe. Here's what that buys you:

1 Starbucks grande coffee, or
2 McDonald's iced coffees, or
2 double macchiatos, or
4 filter coffees, or
4 single espressos, or
4 mugs of instant coffee, or
8 cups of tea

7

What on earth is processed cheese?

'IF IT CAME FROM a plant, eat it; if it was made in a plant, don't,' writes Michael Pollan in his *Food Rules: An Eater's Manual*. Few foods defy this decree more brazenly than processed cheese, yet believe it or not we cannot seem to get enough of the stuff. Processed cheese now accounts for a mind-befuddling 75 per cent of all the cheese consumed in the USA. And before we get on our high horse, it's a similar story in Britain. Despite having access to over seven hundred distinctive regional cheeses (France, by the way, has a paltry four hundred) we get through an astonishing 40,000 tons of processed cheese every year, be it smooth Philadelphia spread, neon-orange Kraft Singles, pots of Dairylea Dunkers or small, individually wrapped Laughing Cow triangles. What on earth is this product that seems to have us in its thrall?

First, some history. No one knows for sure when cheese was first produced but the earliest evidence of cheese making can be found in the village of Kujawy, Poland, where cheese-making equipment dating back to 5500 BC has been uncovered. However, many speculate that cheese is far older. According to one legend, it was discovered accidentally by a nomadic Arabian merchant who at some point around 8000 BC decided to store some milk in a pouch made from a sheep's stomach. As he set out on a day's journey across the desert, the rennet (a series of enzymes found in the stomach of young ruminant mammals) combined with the heat of the sun and caused the milk to separate into curds and whey.

That night the lucky merchant found that the liquid whey satisfied his thirst, and the curd, which had a delightful flavour, satisfied his hunger. In an attempt to preserve this newfangled substance, the resourceful merchant proceeded to salt then press the curd. Thus cheese was born, and the world's taste buds rejoiced.

Believe it or not, the thousands of cheeses we enjoy today, from creamy Brie and rock solid Cheddar to mild mozzarella and stinky Stilton, all start life in exactly the same way. First milk (be it from a cow, sheep, goat, buffalo, camel, reindeer or even, if you're New York artist Miriam Simun, a human) is curdled to separate the solid curds from the liquid whey. To do this, cheese makers usually add rennet. The type of rennet sourced from animals is mostly made up of a coagulating enzyme called chymosin naturally present in the fourth chamber of the stomach of an unweaned calf, kid or lamb. Chymosin essentially turns milk into a soft cheese in the stomach of these young animals so that digestion occurs more slowly and nutrients can be absorbed. So cheese makers use the coagulating property of chymosin just as Mother Nature does, to create curd (albeit in a vat, not a stomach). The curd, which at this point resembles white jelly, is then sliced to release the watery non-coagulated whey (for soft cheeses the curd is cut more coarsely, while for hard cheeses it's cut more finely to allow for the removal of more water). Once the curd has reached the desired consistency it is milled, combined with salt and pressed into moulds to remove any remaining whey. The moulds are then placed in storage rooms where temperature and humidity are strictly controlled and varied according to the style of cheese being made (Cheddar, for example, is named after the Cheddar Gorge in Somerset, where a number of caves provide the ideal humidity and temperature conditions for maturing cheese). Pretty straightforward, then.

Definitions of processed cheese vary wildly, but traditionally the term was used to describe any cheese that had something other than milk, rennet and starter added to it. Prior to the twentieth century most of these ingredients were added to improve flavour and texture. One of the first recipes for processed cheese can be found in a book published in Zurich in 1699 called *Kass mit Wein zu kochen*, or 'To Cook Cheese with Wine' – which, as you may have guessed, suggests melting cheese with white wine and serving it with bread for dipping. The anonymous author had not only invented Switzerland's national dish, the cheese fondue, but also committed to text the recipe for one of the world's first processed cheeses. Other pioneering cheeses soon followed including German kochkäse, made with baking soda and cream, French Cancoillotte, made with the addition of coagulated sour milk and eggs, and, of course, the legendary Welsh rarebit: according to Hannah Glasse's seminal cookbook *The Art of Cookery* (1747), mustard, ale and Worcestershire sauce must be added to the cheese before melting it on toast. And who says British food is bad?

The first commercially available processed cheese wasn't developed until 1911, when Swiss duo Walter Gerber and Fritz Stettler combined shredded Emmental cheese with a preservative called sodium citrate to extend its shelf life when exporting it to warmer countries. Then in 1916 Canadian-born entrepreneur James L. Kraft and his brothers received a patent for 'process cheese' made by heating Cheddar at 80°C for fifteen minutes while whisking it continuously with sodium phosphate. The high heat pasteurized the cheese, helping to extend its shelf life, while the sodium phosphate acted as an emulsifier, giving the cheese a silky smooth texture. The invention helped turn cheese into a shippable commodity and transformed Kraft's company into a cheese-making empire.

Now for the really genius bit. James's brother, Norman, wanted to make things even easier for the consumer by pre-cutting the blocks of cheese into slices. The idea was easier to conceive than to execute: process cheese was packaged and sealed while still fluid and hot; cutting cheese in this state would be akin to slicing syrup. Around 1935, Norman came up with a solution. He poured some liquefied cheese on to a cold stainless-steel table, flattened it out with an iced rolling pin and cut it into even-sized squares which were then stacked on top of one another to create a peelable block. When 'Kraft De Luxe Process Slices' made their debut in 1950, *Modern Packaging* magazine raved that 'all of the handicaps of store-sliced cheese – variations in thickness of slices, slivered edges, imperfect packages, drying out, curled ends, etc. – are overcome'. The *Progressive Grocer* magazine exclaimed, 'many grocers report cheese sales increases as high as 150 per cent'.

DIY: Processed Cheese

Let's face it, when it comes to goo-factor nothing comes close to American-style processed cheese. But why settle for the mass-produced stuff when you can make a gourmet version yourself?

Ingredients

175ml dry white wine	1 tsp salt
190ml water	240g grated Cheddar
2 tbsp citric acid	150g grated Gruyère
1 tsp iota carrageenan	150g grated Gouda

Place the wine, water, citric acid, iota carrageenan and salt in a medium saucepan over a medium-high heat and bring to a simmer, stirring constantly. Keep stirring until it starts to thicken at the edges.

Add the cheeses and whisk until completely melted and smooth. Pour into a nine-by-five-inch silicone loaf tin (or metal loaf tin lined with parchment paper). Refrigerate uncovered for at least two hours, or until the cheese is set.

Remove the cheese from the loaf tin. If not using immediately, wrap completely in parchment paper and then foil. Store in the refrigerator for up to three weeks or in the freezer for up to three months. Once set, the cheese can be grated onto pasta or sliced to top burgers for that deliciously authentic gooey taste.

The cheese single's finishing touch came from outside Kraft. In August 1956 an Indiana-born engineer named Arnold Nawrocki shocked the processed-cheese world with a patent for an 'apparatus for producing individually wrapped cheese slices'. Nawrocki noted that with products like Kraft De Luxe Process Slices and its imitators, the 'cheese slices often stick together, and a consumer has considerable difficulty in trying to separate the individual slices without tearing them'. His machine provided an easy and efficient method for wrapping 'a slice-like slab of cheese in a transparent, pliant wrapper'. Kraft later developed a similar technology, and individually wrapped Kraft Singles were born.

Processed cheese has come on in leaps and bounds since the 1950s and these days you'll find a litany of ingredients including water (which can account for around 56 per cent of the final product), vegetable oil, potato starch, milk proteins like sodium casein (to thicken the cheese), whey powder (a low-cost filler), emulsifying salts like sodium phosphate and sodium citrate (which prevent the cheese from separating when melted), acidifying agents, flavourings, sweetening agents like corn syrup and dextrose, colours like beta-carotene (a natural red-orange food colouring), preservatives and, last but not least, cheese – as in a small amount of curd. This latter ingredient, the one many of us would suppose is the most important, sometimes accounts for a feeble 10 per cent of the final product – just enough to give it a cheesy flavour.

An award-winning artisan food product it is not, but processed cheese has a number of advantages over the real thing. It has a longer shelf life (thanks to the magic of preservatives), it's significantly cheaper to buy (owing to the use of cheap bulking ingredients) and, best of all, it has amazing 'meltability'. Slap a hunk of good-quality Cheddar on top of a burger and stick it under the grill and you can guarantee what will happen: the molten protein gel will separate from the liquid fat. Why? Because water and oil don't mix. Processed cheese is entirely different. Apply a small amount of heat and it melts almost instantly – in fact on a balmy day it will even melt at room temperature – oozing and flowing into all the nooks and crannies of your favourite burger. No drips, no grease, just a warm and tangy topping. This is all thanks to the use of emulsifiers, typically sodium phosphate and potassium phosphate, tartrate or citrate, which reduce the tendency for tiny fat globules in the cheese to coalesce and pool on the surface of the molten cheese.

Sounds good, but is processed cheese technically cheese? In some countries, including Britain and the United States, many processed cheeses cannot legally be labelled simply 'cheese' because of the amounts of additives used during production. Instead they are often referred to as 'cheese food', 'cheese spread' or 'cheese product', depending on the amount of moisture, milk fat and curd present in the final product. So unless the label proudly boasts the word 'cheese', it probably isn't.

8

Does drinking gin make you sad?

TEQUILA MAKES US CRAZY, whisky sends us to sleep, rum turns us into scoundrels, and vodka sneaks up on us like a silent assassin. When it comes to explaining our behaviour the night before, most of us are quick to name-check specific spirits. But one beverage bears the bulk of our blame more than any other: gin, a spirit so infamous it is widely referred to as 'mother's ruin', 'the destroyer', 'the devil', and 'the drink that shall not be named'.

Gin's appalling reputation undoubtedly stems from a period of British history nicknamed the Gin Craze, when consumption of gin in Britain spiralled, frankly, out of control. It all started in the early 1700s when the government began to popularize gin actively as a way to increase trade, prop up grain prices and discourage people from drinking French brandy – something the ruling classes deemed highly unpatriotic. In a cunning move to encourage people to drink more gin (oh, how times do change) the government decided to allow un-licensed production of it while imposing a heavy duty on all imported spirits. The politicians got their wicked way, and by 1726 there were an estimated 1,500 residential gin stills across England and over half of London's 15,000 drinking establishments had been turned into gin palaces – many of which also operated as receivers of stolen goods and prostitutes. The poor, enticed by gin's cut-rate price tag and its reputa-tion as a safer alternative to mains water, flocked to these new bars.

Women were particularly fond of them as they were the first establishments in British history to allow females to drink alongside men.

By 1743 Britain was experiencing a virtual epidemic of extreme drunkenness: the average Briton was getting through a face-ruddying 10 litres of gin per year, and it became plainly apparent that gin was beginning to cause serious social problems. Moral outrage ensued and a host of highly esteemed public figures proceeded to jump on the gin-bashing bandwagon. Radical social reformer Francis Place was first on board, writing that enjoyment for London's poor during this period was solely limited to 'sexual intercourse and drinking', and that 'drunkenness was by far the most desired as it was cheaper and its effect more enduring'. The Middlesex Magistrates got involved too, decrying gin as 'the principal cause of all vice and debauchery committed among the inferior kind of people', while the Bishop of Sodor and Man, Thomas Wilson, complained that gin produced a 'drunken ungovernable set of people'. Even bohemians joined the anti-gin camp. English novelist Henry Fielding blamed gin consumption for increased crime, and Daniel Defoe (a proponent of gin, before things got out of hand) complained that drunken mothers were threatening to produce a 'fine spindle-shanked generation' of children.

The final nail in the coffin for gin's reputation was delivered by the English artist William Hogarth, who in 1751 produced the now notorious engraving *Gin Lane* in support of what would become the Gin Act. Set in the parish of St Giles, a notorious slum district, *Gin Lane* depicts the squalor and despair of a community raised on gin. Desperation, death and decay are rife and the only businesses that flourish are the ones serving or related to the gin industry: gin sellers, gin distillers (the aptly named Kilman), pawnbrokers, and an immensely successful undertaker. Most ominously, the focus of the picture is a woman who, drunk on gin and driven to prostitution by her habit – as evidenced by the syphilitic sores on her legs – lets her baby slip from her breast and plunge to its death in the gin cellar below; the woman is too tanked up to notice, let alone care. Shockingly, Hogarth's character was based on a real woman, Judith Dufour, who a few years before had collected her child from the workhouse only to strangle him and sell his clothes for gin. The engraving, understandably, shocked the public and garnered support for the Gin Act of 1751, which imposed high taxes on the spirit, thus relegating it to the doldrums.

But this is by no means the end of the story. Hogarth's engravings combined with draconian government policies reduced gin consumption for a while, but nothing, it seemed, could deny Britons their favourite tipple for ever.

In tropical British colonies malaria was a persistent problem throughout the 1800s. One particularly effective antidote was quinine, a naturally occurring substance found in the bark of the cinchona tree, which in the early nineteenth century British officers took dissolved in tonic water. To offset quinine's inherent bitterness, these officers took to adding their gin ration, along with a slice of lime, thus inventing one of the world's greatest cocktails: the gin and tonic. This new concoction caught the attention of a more sophisticated clientele (namely those who had the time, money and inclination to drink cocktails in hot climates) and kick-started gin's ascent from the gutters of London to the higher echelons of British society. It might once have ruined mothers (and fathers) and been an early harbinger of binge drinking, but gin had finally become acceptable.

Sadly, the spectre of *Gin Lane* still hangs heavily and the unfortunate spirit continues to be held liable for causing all kinds of untold misery. If gin really can bring us down or send us stir-crazy then what are distillers putting into the stuff to make us feel this way?

Gin, it turns out, is basically a form of flavoured vodka. First a base spirit is made from a variety of different fermentable ingredients such as grain (wheat, rye or barley), grapes, potatoes and sugar cane. This spirit is then infused with botanicals like citrus peel, angelica root, anise, coriander, cinnamon and liquorice root. But it is the juniper berry that gives gin its distinctive fresh, resinous flavour (not to mention its name: the word gin is derived from 'jenever', Dutch for juniper).

Gin: Myths Debunked

1. Gin is a British thing.

Britain may be famous for its huge variety of top-class gins, but the spirit actually descends from a juniper-flavoured liquor called jenever first distilled in Holland and Belgium. In 1618, during the Thirty Years War, England's army saw Dutch soldiers fortifying themselves for battle with jenever and brought this so-called 'Dutch courage' back home with them. When William of Orange, ruler of the Dutch Republic, occupied the British throne with his wife Mary in 1668, gin really took off, particularly in crude, inferior forms, more likely to be flavoured with turpentine than juniper. As for those countries that drink the most gin: Britain comes in at an unimpressive fourth place behind Spain, the USA and the Philippines (who singlehandedly consume half the world's gin).

2. Gin is juniper-flavoured.

While every gin needs to contain juniper berries, that's not the only ingredient used to flavour the elixir. In fact each brand selects its own signature mix of botanicals, which can include a plethora of ingredients, among them lemon peel, anise, angelica seed, orris root, liquorice root, cinnamon, almond, cubeb, savory, lime peel, grapefruit peel, coriander seed, orange peel, dragon eye, saffron, baobab, frankincense, coriander, grains of paradise, nutmeg and cassia bark. Citadelle Gin uses nineteen different botanicals, and Beefeater 24 Gin even calls for Chinese green tea.

3. London Dry Gin is from London.

London Dry Gin, the world's most popular brand, tends to be high in alcohol (around 45 per cent) with a characteristic citrus flavour and aroma due to the addition of dried lemon and/or

(Continued)

orange peel to the botanical recipe. It doesn't need to be made in London (where only a handful of distilleries exist) because gin does not have the same geographical restrictions placed on it as spirits such as cognac, Scotch and tequila. There are, however, thirteen gins that have a 'geographical indication'. The most famous of these is Plymouth Gin, which has been made on the same premises in Plymouth since 1793.

4. Gin and vodka are completely different.
Yes, gin is a spirit made with juniper berries, but gin and vodka start life pretty much the same way: as grain-based neutral spirits. The difference with gin is that it undergoes a final distillation, or sometimes just an infusion, that flavours the spirit with juniper and other botanicals.

5. It's OK to drink a Martini made with vodka.
Of course it's OK, but not if you're a purist. The traditional way to make a Martini is with gin, a smattering of dry vermouth and optional bitters. However, during the 1950s Smirnoff released a very clever campaign, 'Vodka leaves you breathless', which combined with the cool of James Bond to help vodka hijack gin's place in the iconic drink.

Junipers are believed to have a number of health benefits and have been used as an appetite suppressant and a remedy for rheumatism and arthritis for hundreds of years. The juniper berry is also being researched as a possible treatment for diet-controlled diabetes, as it releases insulin from the pancreas – hence its ability to alleviate hunger. However, junipers are not known to cause depression. Even if they did, the amount found in gin after distillation is negligible. On a separate note, orris (the root of the *Iris pallida*, a fairly common garden plant), another ingredient frequently found in gin, is a common allergen. So when people say they are allergic to gin because of the juniper, they may actually be reacting to the orris. But again, sadness is not known to be among its effects.

If juniper berries and orris don't get you down, what other ingredient in gin can? The answer is alcohol – or more specifically, ethanol. Ethanol acts as a disinhibitor, switching off the nerves in the frontal cortex (the bit of the brain that tells us not to be an idiot at the Christmas party). It also acts as a depressant or 'downer' by reducing arousal or stimulation in various areas of the brain. While the immediate effects of alcohol might make you feel happier, long-term use is believed to increase the risk of depression and anxiety. Gin is of course not the only spirit to include ethanol – every alcoholic drink contains the stuff in varying quantities. Therefore any differences in the effect alcohol has on people should entirely depend on the amount of alcohol drunk, the rate at which it is put away, and the mindset of the person drinking it. Not, as many people suggest, the type of spirit drunk.

However, though all distilled spirits contain the same kind of ethanol, around 10 to 20 per cent of the final volume consists of other ingredients, including fusel oils and an organic chemical compound called acetaldehyde. These ingredients are collectively known as congeners and are responsible for most of the taste and aroma of alcoholic drinks. They also happen to vary wildly between different tipples. To establish whether or not congeners can affect us in different ways a study was carried out in 1984. Rats were injected with solutions of cognac, Scotch, tequila, vodka or straight ethanol, then observed for variations in motor impairment. Among the inebriated rats no differences were observed in behaviour or 'rectal temperature' (not sure why they were measuring this). In a similar study on spirits and mood, human subjects were given either bourbon or vodka while living at an inpatient lab for nine days. Researchers noted an increase in anxiety and depression across the board, with no discernible difference between bourbon and vodka drinkers.

These studies seem to imply that all alcoholic drinks affect people in exactly the same way. So what about the millions across the world who say gin makes them feel sad while tequila makes them crazy? Well, there might be a grain of truth in this, but it all comes down to interpretation. In 1999 Swedish social scientist Roland Gustafson gave ninety male subjects beer, red wine, vodka and tonic, or a non-alcoholic placebo version of one of these drinks. Each subject was then seated at a control panel with an electrode strapped to his wrist and told he'd be competing in a series of reaction-time tests against an unseen opponent. The winner of each round would select the intensity of an electric shock to be received by the loser. The whole thing was of course rigged – there was no opponent, and all the subjects 'won' and 'lost' the same number of trials and received shocks of the same gradually increasing intensity. The results? The vodka drinkers subjected their fictitious opponents to stronger and longer-lasting shocks than the beer and wine drinkers did, indicating that high alcohol consumption increases aggression. But (and it is a big but) the placebo vodka had the same effect: subjects who merely *thought* they'd drunk a significant quantity of vodka scored as more aggressive than those who had actually drunk beer and wine. Gustafson's research suggests that drinkers may expect to be affected by different drinks in different ways, and then behave accordingly.

The piece of wisdom to take from this is that if gin is making you feel down in the dumps, it might be because you're expecting it to make you feel that way – thanks in part to the legacy of William Hogarth. This then leads to the self-fulfilling prophecy: because gin is believed to bring you down, people turn to it when they want to feel sad or are in need of a little 'emotional perspiration'. The same theory can be applied to other spirits. Tequila has a reputation for making you rowdy (probably because it's usually drunk in shot form as opposed to being sipped) which means people opt for tequila when they *want* to get a little crazy – and thus its label is confirmed.

Finally, the context within which we enjoy alcohol can also change its effect on us. Port has been blamed for bad hangovers, for example; but when do you drink port except after a four-course meal and about five glasses of wine? Then everyone blames the last drink for their aching head. The same can be said for champagne, a beverage with a reputation for making people exceedingly drunk. (To find out why have a look at chapter 19.) But the chances are the last time you drank champagne was at a party or celebration of some kind, which would generally mean a lot of alcohol was being consumed – often for free, and often on an empty stomach. Again, a gin and tonic is generally something enjoyed on nights out, in a restaurant or at a party, which means you're likely to wake up with a stinking hangover the next day – definitely something that would make you feel down.

You could take heed of Hogarth and shun gin altogether. Just don't go turning to French brandy. That would be terribly unBritish.

9

What is in your doner kebab?

SAY WHAT YOU LIKE about the doner kebab but done well it is truly a thing of wonder: fresh hot pitta stuffed to the gills with juicy ribbons of lamb, crunchy lettuce, fresh tomatoes, onions, and topped off with fiery chilli sauce and a dollop of tahini, maybe even a cheeky scattering of chips to seal the deal. And all for £3.50. Not surprising, then, that the kebab is now one of Britain's most popular takeaway dishes and without a shadow of a doubt our most celebrated après-pub grub.

Not convinced? Then let the statistics do the talking. Around a million kebabs are sold in this country every single day and the British kebab industry now employs an estimated 70,000 people, all responsible for supplying and running the country's 20,000-strong army of kebab shops. In fact the industry is now so profitable it is worth a staggering £2 billion a year, putting it well ahead of burgers, pizzas, sushi and – who'd have thought it? – fish and chips. But how many of us actually know what goes into a kebab? In fact, where on earth do they come from?

Nobody can say for certain where the idea of cooking meat on a skewer came from – let's face it, the method isn't that niche – but legend has it the technique was fine-tuned by medieval Persian soldiers who for the sake of convenience would spear meat with their swords and roast it over an open fire. Unlike in Europe, where whole animals were slowly spit-roasted over roaring fires, these Persians preferred to chop their meat into small pieces and roast them individually over burning embers. The reason for this was entirely practical: small pieces of meat cook a lot quicker than whole cuts, which helps to save fuel – pretty handy in a part of the world with comparatively little firewood. (One of the reasons Britain became the meat-roasting capital of the world was its abundance of woodland, which gave us the luxury of extra fuel for slow roasting.) The trend for cooking meat on swords spread with the nomadic Persians and by the end of the eighteenth century almost every part of the Middle East had developed its own unique variation.

The most radical innovation to the traditional kebab came in the 1860s when Turkish chef Iskender Efendi invented the world's first rotating vertical kebab grill, something he called the doner kebab ('doner' comes from the Turkish verb meaning 'to turn'). It might not sound like a life-changing invention but this newfangled grill changed everything: the meat was healthier because the fat naturally dripped off to the bottom, but more importantly the meat was easier to carve into long, moist, razor-thin slices (complete with a crispy hem) which thanks to the wonder of gravity fell to the plate below. As if Efendi hadn't brought enough to the table, he then proceeded to set the benchmark higher by insisting on using 100 per cent lamb. Prior to this all manner of meats were combined to make a kebab.

Unsurprisingly, this cheap, quick and undeniably tasty way of preparing meat became incredibly popular, and it wasn't long before the doner kebab became well known outside Turkey. Indeed it was in Germany where, according to some, the doner became the thing we all know and love today. In 1972 Turkish immigrant Kadir Nurman opened one of Europe's first kebab shops in Berlin. Until then kebab meat, consisting of roast lamb and spices, had traditionally been served with rice and vegetables, but in a moment of inspiration Nurman saw that the future lay in placing the meat inside a piece of pitta bread – the perfect on-the-go receptacle for busy Berliners. Just forty years later there were the best part of twenty thousand kebab shops in Germany, a thousand in Berlin alone, and the doner is now the country's most popular snack, well ahead of currywurst and bratwurst.

Kebabs were also brought to Britain by Turkish and Greek Cypriots in the sixties and seventies, particularly mainland Turkish immigrants who came to Hackney to work in textiles factories. They first supported the existing kebab shops and later, when their factories closed down, used their entrepreneurial spirit to start their own shops, helping to spread the word of the kebab around the country. A second wave of Turkish and Kurdish immigrants arrived in the late 1980s and helped spur the industry on, particularly in London's East End. Hackney to this day has more kebab shops per mile than any other part of Britain – and, arguably, these doners are the best in the country. But don't tell a Glaswegian that.

So how did freshly cut pieces of meat skewered with a sword become the greyish, congealed elephant leg of nondescript meat we're all used to today? It might be one of the UK's most popular takeaways yet much mystery shrouds the food at the heart of the kebab itself: the doner meat.

Most doner kebab shops don't prepare their own kebabs; the vast majority are pre-made in large-scale processing plants around the country. These plants buy cheap cuts of lamb (like breast and shoulder) that most supermarkets won't use, not because they're dangerous or lacking in flavour but because they have very little retail value. Kebab lovers can take heart from the fact that most of the lamb used in British kebabs is sourced in the UK, which means that not only is your local kebab shop supporting British farmers, the meat has almost certainly been produced with high standards of animal welfare. So no quandaries on the ethical front then.

The meat is then minced and blended with soya protein (a bulker to keep the price down), salt (which acts as both a preservative and an emulsifier) and a whole host of herbs, spices and flavourings like onion powder, garlic, oregano, coriander and nutmeg. After being pummelled in what can only be described as a giant cement mixer, the meat (which at this stage resembles pink ice cream) is then moulded into loaf-like discs and placed by hand on to large metal skewers, one on top of the other. In between each of these discs a layer of lambskin is placed, which when heated helps to bind all the pieces of meat together. Genius. Finally the giant kebabs are trimmed into shape, frozen, wrapped in cellophane and delivered to kebab shops around the country.

Sadly, however, not all doner kebabs are created equal. The huge growth in the popularity of the meal over the last twenty years has seen a proliferation in the numbers of kebab-meat processing plants, making it harder for the authorities to keep tabs on where the meat in your doner comes from and how it is produced. As a result many of the doner kebabs on our streets aren't actually doner kebabs at all. The Food Standards Agency (FSA) says that unless labelled otherwise the meat in a doner kebab must be 100 per cent lamb. An undercover investigation in 2013, however, found that more than two-thirds of the doner kebabs sold in British takeaways are bulked up with other meats (mainly chicken and beef) to save money. When you look at the figures, it's easy to see why. A 10kg bag of lamb kebab meat costs about £35 wholesale, whereas the same pack of lamb with the addition of beef or chicken costs around £15.

But how are these places getting away with it? Though the FSA stipulates that all doner kebabs should be made with 100 per cent lamb, it's up to individual councils to enforce that rule. And the truth is most don't have the time, the resources or the inclination to do so. In other words, it's a kebab lottery out there. Depending on where you live in the country, then, a doner kebab could include reconstituted chicken or beef. Shockingly, some kebab shops have even been found to sell kebabs made with pork, even where the shop claims to be halal. Worse still, in an effort to produce kebabs more cheaply, some producers are pumping their meat full of additional salt and fat, with potentially devastating consequences for our health. While it's safe to say that most people ordering a kebab are not overly concerned with making sound nutritional choices, scientists have found that eating some doner kebabs is akin to dining on a drip tray laden with lard. A study conducted by food standards officers in 2008 found that the average UK doner contains around 140 grams of saturated fat (the equivalent of a wine glass full of cooking oil), 1,000 calories and 100 per cent of the recommended daily allowance of salt.

Think that's bad? That's just the statistics for the average kebab. Some of the worst offenders were found to contain 1,990 calories before salad and sauce (over 95 per cent of a woman's daily calorie intake), 346 per cent of a woman's saturated fat intake and 277 per cent of an adult's daily salt intake – potentially leading to all manner of heart-related diseases. As with the ingredients you find in your doner kebab, how healthy it is seems to depend on where you live. The same study found that the average kebab in the North West averages at just over 1,100 calories, while in London the figure was a relatively modest 912 calories, and Northern Ireland did slightly better than that. As for the South West, this region of the country boasted five of the worst ten kebabs in the whole study.

Let's face it, most of us are not under the illusion that the average doner kebab is good for us, so what is it about them that keeps us going back for more? Alcohol, as you might expect, has rather a lot to answer for. Studies have shown that alcohol actually increases our appetite by suppressing the production of something called leptin, a hormone that normally tells your brain to stop eating. It also, rather famously, makes us lose our inhibitions, making the decision to grab the nearest fast food dish, whatever the implications for our health/reputation, all the more easy. Finally, alcohol wreaks havoc with our blood sugar levels. After just the first drink or two the alcohol rushes into your blood, sending its sugar levels through the roof. This sends an urgent message to the pancreas: 'blood sugar too high, deploy insulin'. The insulin then marches into the blood and escorts the sugar out. As the drinking continues (as it inevitably does) the liver goes into poison elimination mode, its number one mission to remove all toxins from the body. All other duties are scaled down or put on hold, including sending sugar into the blood to balance the efficiency of the insulin. The result? A massive, uncontrollable desire to eat fatty carbs. And we all know what dish can satisfy that urge.

Number Cruncher: Kebabs

£2 billion – amount the kebab industry contributes to the British economy each year

1 million – number of kebabs sold in the UK every day

20,000 – number of kebab shops in the UK

1,101 – calorie content of the average kebab in the North West of England (half a woman's recommended daily intake)

843 – calorie content of the average kebab in Northern Ireland

140 – grams of fat found in the average kebab (nearly 90 per cent of a woman's recommended daily intake and 70 per cent of a man's)

18 – percentage of kebabs found by the UK Food Standards Agency to pose a significant threat to public health

6 – grams of salt found in the average kebab, matching the recommended daily limit set by the FSA

10

What is the difference between green and black olives?

T HE OLIVE IS UNDENIABLY one of the most celebrated fruits of all time. Its taste, virtues and mystique have been praised throughout history in religious texts and by philosophers, poets and writers. But the merits of the humble olive are perhaps best epitomized by English novelist Lawrence Durrell, who once proclaimed: 'The whole Mediterranean, the sculpture, the palms, the gold breads, the bearded heroes, the wine, the ideas, the ships, the moonlight, the winged gorgons, the bronze men, the philosophers – all of it seems to rise in the sour, pungent smell of these black olives between the teeth. A taste older than meat, older than wine. A taste as old as cold water.'

It might sound a little grandiose (especially to those who are not particularly fond of eating olives) but it's hard to overstate the role this fruit has played in shaping human civilization. The Ancient Egyptians traded in olive oil and cured olives as far back as three to four thousand years ago. Their dead were adorned with olive branches and preserved in part with olive oil, and cured olives were left in the tombs of the pharaohs for food in the afterlife. In Ancient Greece the olive tree was considered sacred; its oil was used to anoint kings and athletes and was even used to fuel the 'eternal' flame of the original Olympic games. Victors in these games were then crowned with its leaves. In Greek mythology the goddess Athena brought an olive tree to the Ancient Greeks as a symbol of peace; they, in gratitude, named their capital city after her. By the beginning of the fifth century BC the Romans had invented the screw press – a method of extracting olive oil that remained unchanged for the next two millennia. As the Roman Empire spread, olive trees began to be cultivated throughout the Mediterranean basin, and olive products became a highly profitable item of commerce throughout the Middle East, North Africa and southern Spain. Olives had become a form of currency.

During the Renaissance explorers and colonists began to introduce olives to the New World, including North and South America, Japan, New Zealand and Australia. As a result olives are now one of the most extensively cultivated fruit crops in the world. In a period of just forty years the total cultivation area more than tripled from just over two million hectares in 1960 to nearly eight million in 1998 – more than twice the amount of land devoted to apples, bananas or mangoes. The most extensive olive cultivation is practised in Spain, a country responsible for nearly 45 per cent of the world's olive oil and 35 per cent of the world's table olives. Italy, Greece and Turkey are the other major producers. Together, these four countries account for nearly 60 per cent of the world's olives.

Much of the recent success of the olive can be attributed to our fascination with its array of health-boosting properties. Olives are a rich source of monounsaturated fats. These fats – also found in canola oil, avocados, almonds, hazelnuts and sesame seeds – have been shown to lower harmful cholesterol and help prevent heart disease. Olives can also help to reduce inflammation, a culprit for chronic diseases such as arthritis, asthma, Type 2 diabetes and heart disease, all thanks to a compound found in the fruit called oleocanthal, which prevents the body from making inflammatory enzymes. The list goes on. Olives are rich in fatty acids and antioxidants, chief among them vitamin E, which has been shown to protect skin from ultraviolet radiation, thus helping to ward off skin cancer and premature ageing. Finally, one cup of olives contains around 10 per cent of your daily recommended allowance of vitamin A, which is crucial for healthy eyes.

The health benefits, of course, are not the only reason for the success of the olive. We, like the Ancient Greeks and Romans, love olives for their unique flavour.

As one of the oldest and most important domesticated crops raised by humans, the olive tree has diverged both naturally and with the assistance of man into all manner of varieties. There are hundreds to try, each with its own distinctive, flavourful character. You could fall in love with them for their names alone: rich, smoky Manzanillas from Spain; salty, chewy, jet-black Nyons from the south of France; and, arguably the best, giant, juicy Cerignolas from Italy, which are so big they can be bought brimming with garlic, cheese, peppers, capers or anchovies.

Depending on the cultivator, the shape and texture of olives vary greatly, from tiny spherical orbs to large, plump ovals. Their colour varies as well, but this entirely depends on how long they have been allowed to ripen on the tree. The fruit start out a yellowish green, then during their many months on the tree turn dark green, then light brown, then a dark, mottled purple. Some olives are picked just as they reach their maximum size and just before they begin to turn purple – these are green olives; black olives are those that have been left to ripen further. It is possible to leave them on the tree until they're black (well, dark purple), but that takes a long time, making it impractical on a commercial scale. Olive producers get around the problem by picking olives while they're still green and forcing them to ripen artificially.

First the olives are harvested by hand, usually from October through to January – a slow, gentle, labour-intensive job often done without mechanical devices of any kind. It is with good reason the olives are handled delicately: they bruise easily, with potentially disastrous effects on flavour, appearance and aroma. The Ancient Greeks took this part of the process so seriously that only virgin boys were allowed to harvest olives (how these boys' sexual credentials were proved remains a mystery).

Many people wrongly assume that olives at this stage are ready to eat. Unfortunately for the pickers this definitely is not the case. In fact only two varieties of the 120 or so grown for the table can be eaten fresh from the tree, and they are rarely marketed in the UK. Anybody who has ever tried to eat a raw olive will know they taste disgusting. This is because the skin of an olive contains an extremely bitter compound called glycoside oleuropein. The first man to taste an olive and think it could be turned into something edible must have been a genius – or close to starvation.

There is a theory that in ancient days olive branches overhanging the sea dropped their fruit into the salty waters. After days in the sloshing brine a passing fisherman picked out a bobbing olive and the next thing you know – tapenade! The truth of the matter is that only after long, elaborate curing processes and marinating do olives acquire the palatable taste we are all accustomed to. These processes by which olives are made edible vary wildly: they can be water-cured, oil-cured, dry-cured or even sun-dried, like tomatoes. However, preserving them in brine (salted water) is the most common way to eliminate their bitterness.

The traditional and arguably best way of doing this is to steep the olives in cold water for a period of ten days before submerging them in a strong brine solution for approximately two to three months. During this period they undergo something called lactic fermentation, where the salt in the brine removes the bitter glycoside oleuropein and creates lactic acid, which kills off any existing bacteria. After this the green olives are ready to eat, or to be marinated in oil. The traditional process for making black olives is exactly the same but with one vital difference: after being left to rest in water for ten days they are matured in brine for a minimum of ten months, giving the olives longer to ripen.

The problem with this process is it still takes some time for the olives, green or black, to reach maturity, even if it is only a few months. To save time and money, most mass producers of olives add something to the brine solution called caustic soda, which cuts the maturation period down to a matter of days. Caustic soda, or sodium hydroxide as it's known in the industry, is a poison in its pure form, more commonly used to unblock drains. However, in small food-grade quantities the chemical is safe, and it rapidly penetrates the skin of olives before extracting the bitter oleuropein. It's the use of caustic soda that allows large-scale olive processing plants to produce up to three billion black olives every year.

After the caustic soda treatment the olives are then churned in tanks containing oxidized water to further speed up the ripening process. The olives react with the oxygen in the water and turn a shiny jet black in just a matter of days. The only problem is, the colour isn't for keeps – it will soon fade after the olives are removed from the tanks. To prevent it from fading, a black compound called iron gluconate or ferrous gluconate is added, which reacts with the natural tannins in the olive skin to fix the rich black colour. The final stage for mass-produced olives is either pasteurization (heated to 78°C for five minutes) or sterilization (heated to 125°C for thirty-five minutes) to extend their shelf life.

If it's quicker and saves money, then why don't all producers make olives this way? Well, unsurprisingly, the industrialized way of processing olives doesn't come without its critics. Olive aficionados argue that iron gluconate gives olives a faint metallic taste that is noticeable even after they've been marinated in good oil and aromatic herbs and spices. What's more, most agree that the process of sterilization (something olives produced the slow way don't require) dries olives out and makes them less flavoursome – the sort of olives most of us have probably experienced on top of a frozen pizza.

Mass-produced olives have been blamed for environmental damage too. While some olives are still grown in low-density traditional olive groves, the vast majority are grown far more intensively. The World Wide Fund for Nature argues that olive farming in Europe is turning land to desert, sapping much-needed water and leading to habitat loss for wild species. There is also concern that many mass-produced olives contain high levels of pesticides. Farmers of non-organic olives spray their groves to kill the olive fly pest, often from the air. Aerial spraying can be indiscriminate, affecting other plants and wildlife, and contaminating neighbouring farms.

So, how can you tell whether or not your favourite olives have been treated with chemicals? If the olives have been blackened with ferrous gluconate it should be named on the label, or called E579, or simply 'colouring'. The packaging should also show if the olives have undergone pasteurization. As a rule of thumb, tinned, brined olives are almost always sterilized. Caustic soda, however, is classified as a processing aid and the label will not reveal whether or not it has been used.

Savvy Shopper: How to Buy Olives

Make friends with your local deli: Since labelling doesn't tell us much about curing methods, taste is what we have to depend on. This is one of the reasons it's helpful to buy olives from a deli counter or market stall where you should be given the chance to try before you buy.

Don't be afraid to try something new: There are numerous varieties of olives out there, so lots of room for experimentation. Here are a few to get started with:

- **Oil-cured black olives (Italy, Morocco, Spain):** these shrivelled, wrinkly olives are dry-cured then macerated in oil for several months, giving them their distinctive raisin-like flavour.
- **Cerignolas:** a giant, slightly sweet and fruity variety originating from the southern Italian province of Puglia. Usually served green (though can also be cured until black).
- **Empeltre:** Spanish olives matured on the tree until soft and a lovely glossy purple-black colour. Smooth-textured with a mild, slightly buttery flavour and high oil content.
- **Kalamata:** a large black olive with a rich wine-like flavour from southern Greece. Often used as a table olive and preserved in wine vinegar or olive oil. Kalamata olives have PDO status in the European Union, meaning that only olives originating from that area can be sold as such.

(Continued)

- **Arbequina:** tiny, highly aromatic Spanish olives with a distinctive tangy taste. Mostly grown in Catalonia, but also in Aragon and Andalusia, as well as California, Argentina, Chile and Australia. Particularly good with goat's cheese, feta, dried figs and almonds.
- **Nafplion:** although little known outside Greece, Nafplion olives are some of the most delicious green olives you'll ever try. They have a consistent, firm, crunchy texture and a superb smoky flavour. Particularly good dressed with extra virgin olive oil, slices of fresh lemon and sprigs of dill.
- **Picholine:** a green variety from France with a wonderful nutty flavour. Try them marinated with a little French olive oil and fresh fennel, or as an accompaniment to roast chicken, or seafood dishes.

Make the most of what you've got: A couple of days before serving, poke a few holes in each olive using a cocktail stick then lightly sprinkle them with extra virgin olive oil. Store them in the fridge in a breathable container then serve at room temperature. If you really want to impress, add some grated orange rind, oregano and black pepper.

11

Is sea salt any better than table salt?

IN THE EARLY 1990S most of us had never heard of sea salt let alone seen it. Fast-forward twenty years and you'll be hard pressed to find someone who's never tried it, while TV chefs like Rick Stein, Jamie Oliver and Gordon Ramsay sprinkle it liberally on almost every dish they make (some even use it in their desserts – well, Nigella does anyway).

Their enthusiasm for sea salt, it seems, is contagious. Nearly half the population of Britain now regularly pooh-pooh regular table salt in favour of its upmarket counterpart, while in 2010 alone over 1,350 new food products were released containing the stuff. Furthermore, the per-centage of all foods and beverages containing sea salt has nearly doubled in the last five years alone. And this trend looks set to continue. But why has sea salt become so popular? The truth is, most consumers believe it is more natural, flavoursome and wholesome than table salt – one of the reasons we are prepared to pay up to twenty-two times more for it than normal salt. Is it really worth the price tag?

Paying over the odds for salt isn't a new thing. In ancient times salt was worth its weight in gold – literally. And quite rightly too. Sodium chloride is the stuff of life. Without it we would cease to exist. The sodium found in salt is so important to us it exists in all the body's fluids and is essential to nearly all our bodily functions, including water balance regulation, nerve stimulation and proper function of the adrenal glands. What's more, it is crucial to maintaining normal mental activity: sodium is required to activate glial cells which make up 90 per cent of the brain and are what allow us to think faster and make connections. This is part of the reason why sodium deficiency caused by sunstroke and heat exhaustion leads to confusion and lethargy – the human brain is extremely sensitive to changing sodium levels. No wonder salt was expensive in the past.

But salt isn't just important for our health. It provides us with one of the four (by some counts, five) basic taste sensations (the fifth, according to some, is umami, the taste associated with savoury foods). Not content with imparting its own delectable flavour, salt can enhance the flavours of other foods, too. It does this by increasing the volatility of certain chemical compounds, meaning the molecules are more easily released into the air, and of course aroma is an important part of the taste experience. The wonders of salt don't end there. We might have used canning and artificial refrigeration to preserve food for the last hundred years or so, but for thousands of years salt was the best-known preservative, especially for meat. Indeed, evidence indicates that Neolithic people were boiling salt-laden spring water to extract salt for preservation purposes as far back as 6050 BC.

These days sea salt is harvested around the world in much the same way it was eight thousand years ago (though on a far larger scale, of course) in places like the Île de Ré in south-west France, San Francisco Bay, Cape Cod and the Great Australian Bight. The spiritual home of salt in Britain is Essex, where salt production has been carried out for at least two thousand years. There were two reasons why this coastline was chosen for salt making: a comparatively low local rainfall and the fact that salt marshes mean the tidal waters have a high saline content. At high tide the marshes are covered in seawater; when the tide recedes the salt deposits are left on the drying vegetation and estuary mud. At the following high tide this 'extra' salt is re-dissolved into the tidal waters, resulting in a higher concentration of salt per litre than ordinary seawater.

The method used in antiquity was to allow the tidal rivers to flood basins cut into the clay, which were dammed and then allowed to evaporate naturally. After some time, water from the saline ponds was collected and put into clay pots, which were then boiled over fires. When the process was complete the pots had to be broken to remove the salt. Modern sea salt production uses a pipeline, which draws in water from the sea during the period when salinity is at its highest. The water is pumped into large settling tanks, allowing sediment, mud and other impurities to sink to the bottom. The clean portion of the water is then drawn off and transferred into shallow, open, stainless-steel pans that are heated to boiling point, and the process of salt crystallization begins.

To start with, the magnesium salts float to the surface in the form of a scum. These are removed by skimming. Next, the heat source is adjusted so that the sodium chloride crystals gently begin to form at the bottom of the pans. As more and more water is lost by evaporation the level of the liquid falls and salt crystals begin to form on the surface of the liquid as well. Eventually these become large enough to sink to the bottom. Once a critical amount of sea salt crystals have been formed, they are scooped out, allowed to drain and packaged for sale.

So where does good old table salt come from? The truth is, all salt ultimately comes from the sea; the only difference is that some salt makers use water deposits from today's oceans, while others use deposits evaporated from oceans in previous geological eras. Mined salt (or what many of us today refer to as 'table salt') is extracted from vast sedimentary deposits that have been laid down over millennia as a result of the evaporation of whole seas and lakes. These are either mined directly, producing rock salt, or extracted by pumping water into the deposit – this water is then retrieved with all the salt dissolved in it. In either case, the salt is then purified by mechanical evaporation. Traditionally this was done in shallow open pans which were heated to increase the rate of evaporation; now the process is performed in pans under a vacuum to speed up the process. The raw salt is then refined to

How to Make Your Own Artisanal Sea Salt

It takes time and effort to make your own sea salt, but a little bit goes a long way and there's no replicating the gleam in a food lover's eye when you hand them a hard-earned vial of the finished product. Here's how it's done.

Gather: Visit goodbeachguide.co.uk to find your nearest source of clean seawater. You'll need a lot of water. The rule of thumb is about 20 litres of seawater yields 5 cups of salt, but not all seawater is equally salty, and recent rain showers can skew the ratio. So be prepared for a little trial and error.

Strain: Run the water through a fine sieve or clean cheese-cloth, or both, to catch sand, grit and any other rogue impurities. If you're particular, you can run seawater through a Brita filter (it won't remove the salt).

Evaporate: Put your strained saltwater into a pot and heat on the stove at around 75°C until almost all the water has gone (a 20-litre batch may take a day to evaporate). Once the water level drops to a few inches, salt crystals will start to form. At this point, remove the pot from the heat and carefully pour the water into a wide, shallow pan or Pyrex dish (the shallower the bowl the quicker the remaining water will evaporate). Now leave it on a super-sunny windowsill (yeah, right) or place it in the oven on its lowest setting until all the remaining water has disappeared.

Store: Lightly scrape the salt crystals from the baking dish, breaking up bigger pieces, and store in an airtight container. Your salt is now ready to use.

purify it further. This usually involves something called re-crystallization during which a brine solution is treated with chemicals that remove any remaining impurities (largely magnesium and calcium salts). Multiple stages of evaporation are then used to collect pure sodium chloride crystals, which are kiln-dried.

At this point some table salt manufacturers add iodine. Iodine deficiency is the most common cause of preventable mental impairment, affecting a third of the world's population. It also causes severe thyroid problems. Since 1993 the World Health Organization (WHO) has been conducting a programme of salt iodization to boost dietary levels and prevent deficiency, largely in the developing world. Many European countries, including Switzerland and Denmark, have also signed up to the WHO programme. In the UK, however, it is not compulsory for manufacturers to add iodine to salt.

So, which salt is better? Ask any chef worth their, er, salt why they use sea salt and they'll undoubtedly reply, 'Its flavour.' Laboratory tests show that sea salt has around 1 per cent less sodium chloride than table salt, which is around 99.9 per cent sodium chloride. It doesn't sound like a great deal of difference but the missing per cent is actually made up of minerals like magnesium, calcium and zinc (albeit in microscopic quantities) plus very small amounts of sulphates and even traces of algae. These impurities are one of sea salt's biggest selling points and frequently appear as an identifying mark, such as the tiny bits of clay that give grey sea salt its off-white colour, or the iron-rich red volcanic clay added to Hawaiian sea salt. It is possible that these impurities improve flavour. Since taste and aroma compounds are often detectable by humans in minute concentrations, some say that sea salt has a more complex flavour than just pure sodium chloride. Calcium and magnesium, for example, are known to bestow a faintly bitter overtone, while algae contributes a mildly fishy or 'sea-air' odour. Whether or not you can really detect these flavours in such small quantities remains a matter of opinion. Whichever side of the argument you're on, it might be worth bearing in mind that when sea salt is used during cooking it is highly likely that any subtle flavours will be overwhelmed by other ingredients.

What *can* be proved is that the texture of sea salt has a positive effect on flavour. Table salt, as you will have noticed, is a lot finer than sea salt because it is refined. Each of these tiny crystals of salt is shaped like a cube, meaning you only ever have a sixth of the crystal's surface area in contact with your tongue at any one time. The result is that these crystals take longer to dissolve and release their flavour. Studies have found that the table salt crystals found on most crisps, for example, only dissolve by around 20 per cent in the mouth, and the centre of each tiny cube-shaped crystal remains intact as it makes its way down your digestive tract. Thus a large percentage of the table salt we consume on our food doesn't actually contribute to flavour.

Unrefined sea salt crystals, in comparison, clump together to form large flat pieces like tiny shards of glass. This larger surface area means the salt dissolves a lot quicker, releasing the majority of its salty flavour in the mouth – so you only need to use very small amounts of it to enjoy its flavour. In terms of health some say this is a good thing because it means you use less salt to reap the same benefits in terms of flavour. The human body requires only around a teaspoon of salt a day to stay healthy but most people consume more, usually as a result of eating too many processed foods. In the United States, 77 per cent of the sodium eaten comes from processed and restaurant foods. And eating a diet high in salt is linked with high blood pressure, a risk factor for stroke, heart failure and heart disease. The shape of salt crystals and their effect on our health is taken so seriously that PepsiCo, whose Frito-Lay division makes Lay's crisps, has designed a salt crystal that dissolves completely on the tongue, which should allow each crisp to taste just as salty but with only 20 per cent of the salt currently used.

It isn't all good news for swanky sea salt, though. Far from being healthy, some argue that sea salt is actually damaging our health. Anti-salt campaigners argue that sea salt brands encourage consumers to eat more salt by wrongly claiming it is more natural, wholesome and

Five Things You (Probably) Never Knew about Salt

1. Nesting sea turtles appear to shed tears when laying eggs, but in fact these salty secretions are the turtles' way of ridding their bodies of excess salt consumed at sea. Seabirds don't cry but their bodies contain tiny desalination glands so they never need to drink fresh water.

2. Salt was so valuable during the Roman Empire that soldiers were sometimes paid in it – an allowance they called a 'salarium'. This is where we get the word 'salary'.

3. According to the NHS, we should not consume more than 6g of salt a day. The average Briton consumes over 8g a day, 75 per cent of this intake coming from ready-made foods like bread, cereals, baked beans and biscuits.

4. Only 6 per cent of the world's supply of salt is used in food: 6 per cent is used in agriculture, 8 per cent is used for de-icing streets and motorways, 12 per cent is used in water conditioning and 68 per cent is used to make industrial chemicals, some of which is even used by the aviation industry: jet fuel is combined with salt to remove all traces of water.

5. The high concentrations of salt found in seawater cause fish to lose water through osmosis. To compensate, ocean fish actually drink water through their mouths, excreting the excess salt through cells in their gills. Freshwater fish don't need to drink – they simply absorb water through their skin and gills.

healthy. A recent online survey of 1,358 people found that around one in three admitted to thinking that sea salt is healthier than table salt when in reality both salts contain near identical levels of sodium chloride. The same campaigners also argue that because of sea salt's upmarket image people are likely to use it more liberally, thus increasing their daily intake.

So salt, it turns out, is pretty much salt however much you wrap it up in fancy packaging and bump up the price. But if you really believe sea salt is better, and you're happy to pay up to twenty-two times more for the luxury, that's your choice. Just remember to exercise some moderation.

12

Where does red food colouring come from?

WHEN MOST OF US think of flavour, the first things that come to mind are taste and smell, right? Well, think again. You only have to consider the meteoric rise in the popularity of food blogging, cookbooks and TV-friendly chefs to see there's truth to the adage 'we eat with our eyes'.

According to numerous studies, our habit of *seeing* flavour before we actually taste it starts in early childhood when we begin to associate certain colours with specific types of food, before learning to equate these colours with various tastes. By the onset of adulthood most of us will have brains hardwired to see (and imagine) the flavour of food before we actually taste it; yellow, for example, will likely conjure the taste of banana or lemon, while red will evoke the flavour of cherries or strawberries.

This relationship between food and colour is so engrained in most of us that the unexpected pairing of a given food with an unusual colour can render it inedible. How would you feel if you were served up purple scrambled eggs, green baked beans, yellow bacon and red toast for breakfast? The truth is, most of us would turn it down based entirely on the way it looked, even if we were reassured it was perfectly good to scoff. Not convinced? Subjects in a seminal experiment in the early

1970s were served what appeared to be a normal-looking plate of steak and French fries. The room, however, was installed with special lighting that changed the appearance of the colour of the food. Under this effect, the participants thought the steak and fries tasted fine. But when the lighting was returned to normal it was revealed that the steak was in fact dyed neon blue and the French fries a yucky green. Upon seeing this, many of the subjects refused to eat anything more; some were physically sick.

So enamoured are we with the colour of food, even the most gastro-nomically attuned among us can be fooled by its effects. In 2001, fifty-four sommelier students at the University of Bordeaux fell into the trap of using red wine terms such as chicory, coal, prune, chocolate and tobacco to describe a white wine that had been dyed red – they had pre-viously tasted the same wine in its natural colour and its aroma had evoked honey, lemon, lychee and straw. Funny, that. The same test was later applied to one of Spain's foremost wine tasters, who also fell into the trap (cue smug chuckles).

The power of colour to enhance or weaken our perception of flavour may go some way to explaining why mankind has felt compelled to dye food since time immemorial. Until the discovery of artificial dyes in the 1800s this was achieved using whatever means people could readily find around them. Saffron is mentioned as a colourant for rice in Homer's *Iliad*, and Roman scholar Pliny the Elder remarked that wines were arti-ficially coloured using cinnamon, ginger and elderberry juice as far back as 400 BC. Ancient Romans also used saffron, paprika, turmeric, beetroot extract and the petals of various flowers to enrich the colour of certain foods (all things we still use today). More ominously, in medieval Britain bakers added chalk to whiten bread, and in the nine-teenth century sweet manufacturers loaded their goods with vermilion (which contains mercury), red lead, white lead, verdigris (which is a copper salt), blue vitriol (which contains copper) and Scheele's green (which contains both copper and arsenic). And they say kids these days have a poor diet.

No natural food dye has been more revered through history than carmine, a vivid red dye derived from crushed *Dactylopius coccus*, or the cochineal bug. When Spanish conquistador Hernán Cortés invaded Mexico in 1519 he was amazed to find the Aztec emperor, Montezuma, and other nobles dressed in robes dyed a brilliant red. In Tenochtitlán (now Mexico City) he found the source of this colour: bags of dried cochineal sent as tribute to Montezuma, which he promptly stole and shipped back to Spain. At the time the best red dye available to Europeans was made from another insect, an oak tree pest called kermes (the English colour names 'crimson' and 'carmine' are both derived from the word), which were dried, ground up and dissolved in water. Neolithic cave paintings in France, the Dead Sea Scrolls and the wrappings of Egyptian mummies were all tinted with this dye – a proud history indeed. But compared to cochineal, kermes looked dull.

Cochineal dye was so much brighter than European red dye that it was almost instantly in high demand, and by 1600 cochineal was second only to silver as the most valuable import from Mexico. Around 1630 it was discovered that treating cochineal with an acidic tin solution made it even brighter in colour and bind much better to fabric, giving birth to the first scarlet, as we now know it. Because of its expense and scarcity, scarlet cloth quickly became associated with money and power. Roman Catholic cardinals' robes were made from it, as were the jackets of the British military. Indeed the Revolutionary War in which American colonists fought against these 'Redcoats' was brought on not only by British taxes on tea but also by heavy taxes on cochineal, which could easily have been imported directly from Mexico by the Colonies.

In addition to dye for fabric, cochineal became widely used as a red food colouring. As early as the 1700s cochineal was being used in cakes, jam, jelly, sausages, pies, dried fish, cider and cough syrup. But while ever more diverse uses were found for cochineal, its origin remained a mystery. Most Europeans thought it was extracted from berries or cereals because the dried insects looked like grains of wheat. This misconception was promoted by the Spanish, who launched a fierce cover-up of the dye-making process as soon as they realized cochineal's potential. Access to cochineal farms was tightly controlled and the death penalty invoked against those daring enough to steal the dye. Inevitably, however, French and Dutch adventurers eventually succeeded in smuggling out live insects and cochineal 'ranches' were successfully established in dozens of countries in North Africa, the Mediterranean and the Caribbean. By 1868 the Canaries were exporting six million pounds of cochineal, equivalent to 420 billion insects, a year. This period proved to be the peak of the cochineal industry as new synthetic dyes in a variety of newfangled colours rapidly superseded it. By the early 1900s cochineal production was in steep decline.

Though not in high demand by the clothing industry today, cochineal remains an important colouring for food products and in recent years has even enjoyed a resurgence thanks to its status as an entirely natural dye. As such, these days you'll find cochineal in almost every kind of food requiring a natural red dye including chorizo, jelly, sweets, soft drinks, fruit drinks, chewing gum, dehydrated soups, milkshakes and cakes (it's even used in make-up – yes, if you're female it's highly likely you've worn bug juice on your lips).

But how exactly do you get red dye from an insect? Today, cochineals are harvested mainly in Peru and the Canary Islands on plantations of prickly pear cacti, which the insects penetrate with their beak-like mouthparts to feed on the juices. Because the female insects don't have wings and are sessile (remaining permanently attached in one place on the host plant for the entirety of their lives) they need a powerful defence. That defence is a crimson-hued substance called carminic acid that tastes horrendous to would-be predators such as ants. Fortunately for us, it looks fantastic.

There are two methods of farming cochineal: traditional and controlled. The traditional method involves planting infected cactus pads or infesting existing cacti with cochineals and harvesting the insects by hand. The controlled method uses small baskets called Zapotec nests

In the Know: Cochineal Insects

Cochineal insects are small plant-sucking 'scale' insects closely related to the aphid but not at all related to beetles as most people think. (The term 'cochineal beetle' is a complete misnomer.) They are native to tropical and subtropical South America and Mexico, where they live on cacti of the genus *Opuntia*, feeding on plant moisture and nutrients.

There are over twenty families of scale insects comprising nearly eight thousand species and in most of them the female is sessile and produces carminic acid to protect itself, especially from ants.

The carminic acid is extracted from the body and eggs, by drying then crushing the insects, before being mixed with aluminium or calcium salts to make carmine dye, also known as cochineal. Making just one kilo of the red food dye requires around two hundred thousand insects. The carmine is primarily used as a food colouring and for cosmetics, especially as a lipstick colouring.

Though carmine is considered a safer alternative to synthetic food dyes, it doesn't come without its downsides. A small number of people have been found to have an allergy to it, with effects ranging from mild cases of hives to asthma attacks and even anaphylactic shock. For obvious reasons the use of carmine dye in food is generally unacceptable to vegetarians and vegans but also to Muslims, who consider anything derived from insects a *haraam* (forbidden) food.

containing fertile females that leave the nests and settle on the cacti to await fertilization by males. After mating, the fertilized female increases in size and gives birth to tiny nymphs. It's the crushed bodies of these female insects and their nymphs that produce the red pigment. The new cochineals are left to reproduce or are collected and dried for dye production. Harvesting the insects is labour-intensive as they must be individually knocked, brushed or picked from the cacti by hand before being placed into bags by small groups of collectors who sell them to local processers or exporters. The insects are then sun-dried, crushed and dunked in an acidic alcohol solution to produce carminic acid, the pigment that eventually becomes carmine or cochineal extract.

Until 2009 cochineal was one of many dyes that fell under the umbrella term 'natural colour' on ingredients lists. But because cochineal provokes severe allergic reactions in some people, many countries (including the UK) now require carmine and cochineal extract to be explicitly identified. So any time you see an ingredients list that includes the words 'carmine', 'cochineal extract', 'crimson lake', 'C.I. 75470', 'natural red 4', 'E120' or even 'natural red', you can be sure that there's a little powdered bug therein.

Don't like the sound of an insect-induced allergic reaction? Synthetic red dyes can carry even greater health risks. Some artificial food colouring these days comes in the form of a petroleum-derived chemical called Allura Red AC or E129. In 2004 a team of researchers from Southampton University found strikingly increased levels of hyperactivity and attention deficit disorder in children consuming artificial food dyes (including Allura Red), which is one of the reasons the dye is banned outright in Denmark, Belgium, France and Switzerland – though it isn't in the rest of Europe and the USA. Makes insect juice sound positively appetizing.

DIY: All Natural Food Colouring

Crushed insects and petroleum-derived chemicals don't float your boat? Why not have a go at making your own natural food colouring at home? It's easier than you think . . .

Yellow: Both saffron and turmeric create a vivid yellow. But beware, these spices are extra strong and a little goes a long way, so start small and test as you go. Try making natural yellow cake icing by replacing the water called for in a recipe with saffron-dyed water. Place some saffron in a small bowl and crumble it with your fingers. Then pour a few tablespoons of hot water over it, stir, and let it sit for a while until the colour deepens.

Orange: Carrots are your best bet (citrus fruits might seem tempting but they don't lend much colour). Juicing them is the most effective method but if you don't have a juicer just buy some fresh 100 per cent carrot juice. The best thing? Carrot juice is naturally sweet, reducing the need to add sugar. Try making orange frosting by mixing half a teaspoon of carrot juice per two tablespoons of frosting.

Red and pink: With a load of colour and almost no flavour, beetroots are perfect for the job. Use the juice from the canned/vacuum-packed kind, or make your own by either boiling or juicing the raw vegetable. For a lighter pink and a bit more flavour use red berries like raspberries or strawberries. These will impart their own taste – not necessarily a bad thing when it comes to cake. To procure your dye, pulverize the berries in a food processor or blender then strain out the coloured liquid using a mesh sieve or cheesecloth.

Green: Mash, process or otherwise obliterate the flesh of half an avocado. This will lightly colour a cup or two of icing. Avocado has an understated flavour so it won't dominate the

(Continued)

dish. Alternatively, purée half a cup of fresh or frozen spinach. Boil it in four cups of water and then simmer for a couple of hours. When it's concentrated, strain out the spinach – it's the liquid you want. Add the concentrate to your recipe. Another option for an emerald tone is liquid chlorophyll (available at health food shops), which aside from being a 'healthy supplement' will impart an awesome emerald tint to your food.

Purple and blue: Purple is pretty straightforward and is achieved by boiling red cabbage until you get a dark, concentrated broth. To make blue food dye, make your purple dye as above but add a bit of baking soda at the end. Slowly stir it through and watch, stunned, as it reacts with the cabbage juice and miraculously turns blue.

13

How safe is it to eat oysters?

N O FOOD IS CAPABLE of creating a taste sensation quite like an oyster. Eating one is a uniquely invigorating experience that miraculously conjures the briny, face-thwacking essence of the sea in sublimely simple, portable form – it's nature's seafood ready-meal but with oodles more class than your average filet-o-fish. No surprise then that oysters are enjoyed almost everywhere on the planet from the thunderous, rocky coast of the Cape of Good Hope to the chilly northern waters of Nova Scotia. Britain alone boasts dozens of delicious species from silky, sweet Colchester Natives to crisp, cucumber-like Caledonians.

Not only do the flavours of oysters vary widely, so too do the ways in which we enjoy them. Some reduce them to receptacles for downing chilli sauce. Others pair them with pints of porter or even combine them with vodka, vinegar, ketchup and horseradish to make a fiery cocktail. In Virginia's Chesapeake Bay, locals bake them with onions, breadcrumbs, celery and eggs to make a turkey stuffing. Certain molecular chefs serve their oysters on a bubbly cloud of vaporized sage with a fizzy hit of parsley champagne (no, me neither). Some prefer theirs poached, grilled, fried, stewed, smoked, boiled, pickled or, in New Orleans, smothered in butter and cheese and stuffed into a Po' Boy sandwich (the travesty!). A small – but misguided – number of people believe oysters will guarantee a good time in the sack, and couldn't care less how they are served. But a traditionalist opts for his oysters pure and unadulterated – a bracing hit of the sea delivered straight from its pearly shell. Yet however or wherever you choose to enjoy an oyster, one belief is universally acknowledged by nearly all who eat them: with every briny mouthful there is the risk of a dodgy stomach, full-blown food poisoning, or maybe even death. But does the humble oyster deserve such infamy?

If looks are anything to go by, it's understandable why oysters have garnered such a bad reputation. 'It was a bold man who first ate an oyster,' said eighteenth-century satirist Jonathan Swift. Yet at some point in history somebody did take the plunge for us all and tried one. We don't know who this person was, but we have a pretty good idea of where he came from: a cave at Pinnacle Point along the southern coast of South Africa, where scientists have found evidence of human oyster consumption from 164,000 years ago. It is here, experts believe, that the first human prised open an oyster with the help of a flint and guzzled down its slimy contents. Upon realizing it did him no harm, the pioneering gourmand promptly gathered more. They were abundant, easy to gather, required no cooking whatsoever, and were delicious. What was there to stop the trend for oyster eating spreading?

By the time the Romans invaded Britain in AD 43 Britons had long regarded shellfish, particularly oysters, as something of a subsistence food, handy to have in times of need but never to be sought when there was fish or meat to be had. The Romans, however, brought with them an enthusiasm for eating shellfish as a culinary treat, and once the military invasion was over and traders and civilians began to arrive from across the empire, oyster farming flourished. Indeed so revered were British oysters they were regularly exported back to Rome. The shells of oysters (along with whelks, cockles, mussels and limpets) are still found extensively on the sites of Roman villas, towns and forts as far north as Hadrian's Wall, not only near the coast but also great distances inland – presumably the oysters were transported alive in water tanks. Liberal consumption of oysters in Britain continued into Victorian times, when pickled oysters were an everyday food for the poor of London and other industrial towns. As Dickens' character Sam Weller remarks, 'Poverty and oysters always seem to go together.'

The types of people frequenting oyster bars nowadays may have changed since Roman times but the ways in which we rear them have barely altered an inch. As in AD 43, wild oysters are transferred to sheltered inland estuaries where they are left to spawn. Once the stock has reached the correct weight and size (which may take a number of years depending on the species) they are dredged from the estuary bed using mesh cages and sorted by hand. Unlike many other modern aquaculture practices (namely salmon farming), oyster farming is generally considered to be positively beneficial to a marine environment. Oysters are heavy drinkers, gulping down an average of 200 litres of water a day in their attempt to extract nutrients from the sea. As such they provide a free cleaning service to the inhabitants of coastal towns, filtering out any excess nitrogen. An oyster's voracious appetite for seawater is what gives it its intense flavour. As the thirsty mollusc filters litre after litre of water it also accumulates concentrations of algae and various minerals unique to its location, meaning that oysters, like wine, carry their provenance like an edible fingerprint.

The bad news is, seawater isn't always clean; it can be riddled with all kinds of things you wouldn't want to put inside your mouth, let alone your stomach, including sewage and agricultural chemicals. Therefore as well as delicious minerals oysters accumulate bacteria and viruses, especially in areas at risk of pollution. Because of this nearly all oysters carry the risk of food poisoning. In America several people die each year as a result of eating raw oysters contaminated with the potentially deadly *Vibrio vulnificus*, a naturally occurring bacterium belonging to the same family of bacteria as the causative agent of cholera. But with only about thirty cases in the United States a year, it's exceptionally rare: your chances of finding a valuable pearl in one of the 2.5 billion oysters Americans eat every year are about a hundred times greater than your chances of becoming infected with the bacteria. Nevertheless, when *V. vulnificus* strikes, it strikes hard, on a global basis killing about half the people who get it. And many of these deaths are usually exceedingly grim. According to the US Food and Drug Administration, those most at risk are individuals with liver damage or disease, diabetes, cancer, stomach disorders or any illness or ailment that weakens the immune system.

When it comes to waterborne nasties, British oysters fare little better. In a study conducted by the Food Standards Agency in 2011 it was found that 75 per cent of fresh British-grown oysters taken straight from their rearing beds contained some level of norovirus, the cureless stomach bug that most of us know as the 'winter vomiting bug' – yes, the one that causes explosive bouts of diarrhoea and projectile vomiting. The trouble with norovirus is it's highly contagious. Once someone with it has been sick, a fine mist of vomit remains suspended in the air before settling on the table, the cat, the cushions, the TV or any other object in the infected person's vicinity. If someone enters this room there's a high chance they'll catch it too. Just one of the reasons why between six hundred thousand and a million Brits succumb to the virus every single year.

If eating oysters is tantamount to playing Russian roulette with a norovirus-shaped bullet, why are more people not falling ill? After all, thousands upon thousands of oysters are eaten every single day. The truth is only a relatively small number of people catch norovirus or other similar bugs as a direct result of eating oysters. This is partly thanks to the FSA, which requires oysters to be purified before being sold. Purification entails placing oysters in tanks of clean seawater for a minimum of forty-two hours to purge any microbiological contamination they might have accumulated while in their natural environment. During this time the seawater is treated with UV light (to disinfect it) and aerated (to mimic the conditions of the oyster's natural habitat). Once placed in these tanks the oysters resume normal filter-feeding activity and excrete contaminants in their faeces, which falls to the bottom of the tank and is then removed. By enabling the oysters to self-clean in this way the risk of their carrying the dreaded norovirus is reduced. It should, however, be pointed out that though purification is thought to be effective, testing oysters is notoriously difficult, meaning no one can be 100 per cent sure they are virus-free. In short, oysters will always have the potential to make you ill, no matter how small the odds may be.

As for the old adage that oysters are safe to eat in months containing the letter 'R' . . . there might be a grain of truth in this pearl of folk wisdom. Months without the letter 'R' in their names (i.e. May through to August) coincide with summer in the northern hemisphere. These warmer months, historically, made for bad or even toxic oysters for a couple of reasons: first, in the days before refrigeration shellfish were more likely to spoil in the heat; second, the toxins that cause waterborne sickness multiply more rapidly in warmer waters, making their way into the plankton that oysters eat. But now that all oysters are purified, this risk is reduced. The other negative effect months without the letter 'R' have on oysters is a decrease in flavour. The summer months mark spawning season for oysters, and since most of their energy goes towards reproduction, the oysters' meat is likely to become fatty, watery, soft and less flavourful, as opposed to the more desirable lean, firm texture and bright seafood flavour of those harvested in cooler, non-spawning months.

If oysters can potentially contain harmful bacteria or viruses at any time of the year, is it worth the risk? Though there's a very small chance that eating oysters can make you ill, the general consensus is that the health benefits of consuming them far outweigh the risks. Raw oysters nutritionally consist of around 23 per cent carbohydrates, 33 per cent fat and 44 per cent protein, making them an exceptionally balanced food and a great source of omega-3; they're also a good source of zinc, selenium, vitamin D, iron, magnesium and phosphorus. Perhaps of equal importance, raw oysters have always been linked with a great sex life. Aphrodite, the Greek goddess of love, sprang forth from the sea on an oyster shell, promptly gave birth to Eros, and the word 'aphrodisiac' was born. Casanova, the renowned eighteenth-century lover who admitted in his memoirs to seducing 122 women, famously used to breakfast on fifty oysters. Old wives' tales have long proclaimed that eating raw molluscs, oysters in particular, will stimulate your libido.

Until recently this relationship between oysters and libido had been dismissed as mere myth. But studies have now shown that oysters help men to refuel on zinc, a highly beneficial element lost through ejaculation. Furthermore, in 2005 a team of Italian researchers analysing bivalve molluscs – a group of shellfish that includes oysters – found they were rich in rare amino acids that trigger increased levels of sex hormones. The scientists stressed that oysters have to be eaten raw to be most effective. If that isn't reason enough to gulp down a dozen, what is?

In the Know: How to Eat Oysters

Know your species: There are two types of oysters widely consumed and available in the UK: the Pacific (or rock) oyster and the native (or flat) oyster. The Pacific oyster was introduced to Europe around thirty years ago to boost stocks. It is cheaper than a native oyster because it grows quickly and can reach palatable size in around two years (compared with four for a native). It has the same succulence as natives, but many prefer the more complex flavours and firmer texture of natives.

Get experimental: Different oysters suit different occasions and different people. If you haven't yet been wowed by them, you may well have been eating the wrong ones. There are oyster fisheries all around Britain; particularly well-known beds lie off Essex, Kent, Dorset, Devon, Cornwall, the west of Scotland and Ireland. Each region's produce differs in flavour. Maldon oysters, for example, are smooth and meaty with a distinctly citric tang, Whitstable oysters are lauded for their saline, silky plumpness, and a Poole oyster is said to taste of pecan nuts and avocado.

(Continued)

Choose the right moment: Remember, there is some truth to the saying that oysters should not be eaten during months that do not contain an 'R'. While oysters are still safe to eat from May through to August, it's likely they won't be at their best because it's the spawning season: the meat is likely to become a little watery and less flavourful.

Exercise some quality control: The key to a good oyster is freshness. It should smell of fresh sea air, have a firm texture and be brimming with natural juices. The heel of the oyster, in the deep part of the shell, should be a creamy ivory colour. The frill should be moist and pulsating, and the oyster should always look bright and sparkly. If the shell isn't firmly closed it should do so immediately when tapped.

Learn to shuck: Oysters don't always have to be enjoyed in a restaurant. In fact it's way more fun – and a damn sight cheaper – to enjoy them at home. The tough bit is getting them open. Buy a shucking knife with a short, strong blade and insert it into the hinge of the oyster (the small opening at its most narrow end). Then carefully work the knife around the circumference of the oyster shell (this will require a fair amount of wiggling) taking care not to spill any juice. Finally, twist the knife to prise open the shell then release the oyster from the shell by cutting the abductor muscle. Serve chilled, on crushed ice.

Get slurping: There are those who insist on swallowing oysters whole. Some consider this a crime. Oyster flesh has a wonderful texture and, like a piece of meat, releases its flavour when lightly chewed. Purists take them as they come, perhaps with a squeeze of lemon or a dash of Tabasco sauce, but if you're not keen on raw shellfish they can be lightly grilled, fried, or baked in a little sauce.

14

What exactly is scampi?

OF ALL THE BILLIONS of questions typed into internet search engines by curious Britons every year, what would you say were the most common? 'Who wrote the Magna Carta?', 'Which monarch established the Church of England?' or 'When did the Romans invade Britain?' Well, how about 'What is scampi?' Bizarrely, this last question turns up more search results than any of the other three biggies. It seems that while we enjoy eating £50 million worth of these deep-fried fishy nuggets every year – served, preferably, in a mock-wicker basket replete with chunky chips, a wedge of lemon and a dollop of tartare sauce – few of us know precisely what they are or where they come from. Some believe scampi to be simply another word for 'prawns', others say it's a type of scallop. There are even those who posit that a scampi is a mysterious variety of sea animal (a bit like those who believe the Scottish haggis to be a furry moor-dwelling rodent replete with tartan tam o' shanter). The truth, of course, is more complex than any of these suggestions – and a whole lot more interesting.

First, the basics. To cut to the chase: scampi is in fact a made-up consumer-friendly name to describe the deep-fried tails of a group of rather ugly beady-eyed crustaceans called *Nephrops norvegicus*, known variously as the Norway lobster, the Dublin Bay prawn or the langoustine. Think of it as the smaller cousin of the lobster, caught mainly by trawlers in the North Sea, Irish Sea and off Scotland's west coast. These orange-pink scavengers were ingeniously renamed 'scampi' in 1946 by Young's Seafood, the UK's leading frozen food manufacturer, as a way to make what was a highly under-utilized shellfish sound more appealing to picky consumers. As for the name, it isn't British at all. The word 'scampi' is simply the plural version of the Italian word 'scampo', which means 'prawn'. Why exactly Young's chose an Italian word remains a mystery but it certainly struck a chord: by the 1970s scampi and chips served 'in the basket' had become Britain's most popular pub snack.

Indeed this once unsellable crustacean has become so enduringly successful it is now one of the most valuable and lucrative species of sea creature landed at UK harbours, worth a staggering £97 million each year. Some 60,000 tons are caught annually, half of them in UK waters. More impressive still, the made-up name has stuck and langoustine tails are invariably referred to as scampi across the UK. In fact the name scampi is now so engrained in British culture the word *Nephrops* isn't even required on scampi packaging. Pretty understandable, really: 'I'll have a pint of bitter and a basket of *Nephrops norvegicus*' just doesn't cut the mustard.

Unfortunately, as demand for langoustines has risen, so has their price. So revered are British langoustines right now that many of the largest whole specimens are sold to European fishmongers, often in France and Spain, as a luxury seafood. These are then ferried off to upmarket restaurants in Paris and Barcelona, where with the help of a lick of butter and a star anise jus they can fetch upwards of £20 a serving (yes, that's right: a large proportion of the nation's most important and tastiest seafood is being ferried the length of the country and whizzed across the Channel with hardly any being kept for our own market). The whole langoustines that manage to remain on our shores aren't much cheaper. Buy a batch from your local fishmonger and you could be forking out as much as £40 a kilo.

With prices like this how come you can find a portion of whole breaded scampi tails at your local supermarket for less than £10 a kilo?

Well, it all comes down to the type of langoustines used and the way in which they're processed. Off the west coast of Scotland, langoustines are often bred in lobster pots to ensure undamaged premium products to export – it is these that are likely to end up on the dinner plates of European gourmands. The langoustines used to make pub scampi, on the other hand, are most commonly trawled en masse using huge nets, which often results in the capture of smaller specimens which more often than not have damaged claws and shells. These no-thrill langoustines have their heads and claws removed at sea before being whisked off to processing plants on the mainland where they are de-shelled. Traditionally this would have been done by hand but to save money the vast majority of plants use automated de-shelling machines – a great way to save money and lower the cost for frugal consumers. Unfortunately, mechanized de-shelling (like trawling en masse) damages the langoustine. Rare are the langoustine tails that survive this somewhat brutal process intact. Luckily for those of us who insist on our 'whole tail scampi' being perfectly formed, the damaged bits of tail are then bound together to ensure a consistent shape, size and weight. Individual processing plants produce a staggering 86 tons of affordable scampi every week in this way.

But there's another kind of scampi on the market that offers consumers even more for their money. These are known as 'scampi bites' and can cost as little as £1.49 a bag (or £6.35 per kilo). Those readers who have eaten one of these bad boys will know exactly what they are: perfectly spherical balls of spongy, grey-looking flesh entombed in a thick, greasy jacket of breadcrumbs. Squeeze them between your fingers and a torrent of fishy water will spew forth. These little beauties are in fact a type of re-formed processed food made with a blend of langoustine tails, preservatives and anonymous 'flaked white fish', often glued together using an additive called sodium tripolyphosphate, or STPP for short. This chemical is commonly used in clothing detergents and anti-freeze. In the seafood industry, however, it's used in small food-grade quantities and it makes reconstituted fish and shellfish appear firmer,

Know Your Langoustines

The Great British public have been chomping on these little critters for the best part of half a century, but most of us haven't the faintest idea what they are. Time to get truly acquainted . . .

Name: *Nephrops norvegicus*, known as the Norway lobster, Dublin Bay prawn or langoustine.

In a nutshell: A slim, orange relative of the lobster that can grow to about 24cm in length. Hugely popular in Spain and widely used in classic French cuisine. Scampi is the name for deep-fried langoustine tails, though confusingly other prawns and fish cooked similarly may be sold as 'scampi' too. They are most often served deep-fried in batter and breadcrumbs, with chips, peas and tartare sauce, but you may also find them cooked whole, boiled or steamed.

Distribution: Found in seabed burrows in the north-eastern Atlantic Ocean and North Sea, as far north as Iceland and northern Norway, and south to Portugal.

Biology: Males grow relatively quickly to around 6cm, but seldom exceed ten years old. Females grow more slowly and can reach twenty years old. In the autumn females lay eggs that remain attached to the tail for up to nine months (known as being 'berried'). During this time the berried females rarely emerge from their burrows and therefore do not commonly appear in trawl catches – one of the reasons langoustines have remained somewhat resilient to fishing pressures. Egg hatching occurs in the spring, and females emerge then to moult and mate.

(Continued)

> **Sustainability:** Trawler-caught langoustines have been associated with large quantities of by-catch, including overfished species such as cod and juvenile fish. Increase the sustainability of the scampi you eat by choosing pot- or creel-caught rather than trawled scampi. If choosing trawled fish, ask for langoustines trawled in nets using 'separator grids' and larger meshes to increase their selectivity and reduce by-catch and discards.

smoother, glossier. It also causes the flesh of seafood to absorb water. Bulking seafood out in this way makes scampi cheaper to produce and buy – though it doesn't take a brain surgeon to figure out that pound for pound you get less actual seafood for your money. In fact some tests have shown certain scampi bites to contain more water than actual langoustine. Along with cheap scampi, some of the more common seafood items 'soaked' in STPP include scallops, prawns and anything filleted that's particularly flaky, like hake, sole or imitation crab meat.

Shockingly, no minimum amount of langoustine is required for a product to be called a 'scampi bite'. In fact you can flog any old fish nugget as a 'scampi bite' as long as it contains at least a trace element of langoustine in its recipe. The total fish content of some supermarket scampi bites is often as little as 7 per cent, the rest being breadcrumbs, brine, water and a cocktail of other ingredients that has been found to include ascorbic acid (an antioxidant and colour stabilizer), anti-caking agent (to prevent the formation of a lumpy batter), disodium diphosphate (a chemical preservative), xylose (a sweetener) and potassium carbonate (an ingredient often used in gunpowder but used by the food industry as a baking agent).

As for the 'white fish' used to bulk out scampi bites, this can be almost anything. Traditionally scampi producers used monkfish tails, but now that these are considered a premium product you're much

DIY: Scampi and Chips

Sweet, juicy lobster-like flesh encased in an intensely moreish, crunchy batter ... proper scampi is a thing of wonder. The trouble is, not all of the stuff you can buy in the shops comes close. Some is bulked out with water, reconstituted white fish and a whole host of unappealing additives. All the more reason to have a go at cooking it yourself. I like mine with a bit of a kick, but you can leave out the cayenne pepper and paprika if you prefer.

Serves 2

2 large potatoes, preferably
   Maris Piper, cut into chunky
   chips
1 tsp cayenne pepper
1 tbsp olive oil
8–10 raw peeled langoustines

2 free-range eggs, beaten
140g dried breadcrumbs
1 tsp paprika
tartare sauce and lemon wedges,
   to serve (optional)

Preheat the oven to 180°C/gas mark 6. Arrange the chips on a baking tray, drizzle with the oil and season. Bake for 40–45 minutes until golden, turning halfway through.

Season the breadcrumbs with the cayenne pepper and paprika. Mix the langoustines in the beaten egg, lift each one out with a slotted spoon so that any excess egg drains off and toss them in the breadcrumbs until coated. Transfer to a baking tray.

When the chips have 10 minutes to go, heat grill to high. Cook the langoustines for 3–5 minutes each side, until crisp and cooked through. Serve with the chips, some tartare sauce and lemon wedges.

more likely to find clusters of something called 'reconstituted white fish matter' in with your langoustine. In more expensive brands this can be made up of hake, cod and haddock, but those at the value end of the spectrum are more likely to incorporate cheaper, more exotic-sounding species from around the world, including Alaskan pollack (most of which is shipped from China where it is sent for reprocessing), Nile perch (a species of freshwater fish found in East Africa), tilapia (a freshwater fish usually farmed in Thailand) and pangasius (a humongous river-dwelling catfish farmed in Vietnam). Whether or not scampi bite brands should be allowed to label these freshwater fish species as 'white fish' remains a matter of debate; traditionally the term applies to marine fish only. Furthermore, white fish is often associated with wild-caught fish, while perch, pangasius and tilapia are all farmed.

While definitions of the ingredients found in scampi remain somewhat fuzzy, one thing consumers can be sure of is that with an Italian name and an ingredients list boasting fish from Africa, China and South East Asia, scampi bites are one of Britain's most multicultural dishes. Not bad for a humble bit of pub grub.

15

How much cow is in beef stock?

STOCK MAKING IS AN ancient practice that is probably as old as cooking itself, the invention of a thrifty and resourceful Neolithic ancestor who decided to taste the water left behind after cooking meat, fish or vegetables and wisely deduced that the hot broth must have absorbed some of the food's flavour and goodness. It is this basic principle that continues to influence the many and varying styles of stock making we see today. In Japan a fish and kelp stock called dashi is made by briefly cooking skipjack tuna (bonito) flakes called *katsuobushi* in nearly boiling water. In Italy, and many other parts of Europe, mineral-packed chicken stock is still eaten as a cure for the common cold. Professional chefs create stocks made with gelatin-rich bones to set terrines and make rich syrupy jus (or posh gravy to you and me). In France stock – or *bouillon* as it's known there – isn't just an accompaniment, it's the body and soul of many of the country's most revered dishes from the lowliest slow-cooked casserole to the chicest Michelin-starred sauce.

You may not believe it but stock making has a proud history in Britain, too. One of the country's oldest recipes, dating back to 6000 BC, is nettle pudding – essentially a thick syrupy stock with large herby dumplings (an easy form of carbohydrate in an age when potatoes would not be around for another fifteen centuries or more) boiled in the same water as a joint of meat. Stock is also a central ingredient in what is arguably Britain's most popular dish of all time: pottage, a type of stew made by boiling vegetables and grains in the juices of meat or fish. Pottage was so popular it was pretty much the staple food of all Britons from Neolithic times right up until the Middle Ages. Our love of stock continued through the centuries, and in the 1800s Yorkshire folk began to combine the juices of slow-cooked beef with flour, water and herbs, thus inventing 'proper' gravy – and where would we be without that? As for vegetarian stock, we had that one covered too. In her cookbook *Good Things in England* (1932), Florence White wrote: '[The soup] is nothing more than the water in which young cabbage has been boiled . . . It is extremely good and delicate and tastes very much like chicken broth. It is not merely an economy but a luxury; one of the best of health and beauty drinks.'

In recent times, however, the long-established art of stock making appears to have been banished from the average kitchen, along with other ancient culinary crafts like curing meat, churning butter and baking bread. All deemed too laborious, complex and time-consuming for the modern home cook. The UK's most popular chefs are obviously aware of this. Look at any recipe requiring stock and the chances are you'll find some reassuring words along the lines of 'you can find this at your local supermarket'.

Chief culprit in the demise of traditional stock making has been the meteoric rise of meat extract, a highly concentrated pre-made stock invented by the eminent nineteenth-century German chemist Baron Justus von Liebig. Fuelled by a desire to help feed the undernourished, in 1840 Liebig developed a concentrated beef extract he proudly named *Extractum carnis Liebig*, to act as a nutritious meat substitute for those unable to afford the real thing. A recipe for Liebig's original creation can be found in Robert Kemp Philip's seminal book *Enquire Within Everything* (a sort of Victorian how-to book for general domestic life): 'Take a pound of good juicy beef from which all the skin and fat has been cut away, chop it up like sausage meat; mix it thoroughly with a pint of cold water, place it on the side of the stove to heat very slowly, and give an occasional stir. It may stand two or three hours before it is

The Ten Cardinal Rules of Stock Making

1. Break the bones and cut up the meat. This will help to intensify the flavour of your stock.

2. Start with cold water and bring to a simmer slowly. Don't boil. As the water gradually heats, the flavours will leach out (as opposed to boil away) and any connective tissues will break down, releasing their gelatin, which acts as a thickener.

3. Avoid tomato, cabbage, broccoli, cauliflower and too much celery as these have a tendency to overpower the overall flavour; but do use a stick of celery along with some carrot, onion, a clove or two of garlic, a few bay leaves and even a bouquet garni. Steer clear of pork, too, as this is very fatty.

4. Never add salt. What seems like a good amount of salt now will be significantly stronger by the time you're done.

5. The amount of water you use depends on the size of your pot. Arrange the ingredients in your pan with as few gaps as possible then add just enough water to cover everything.

6. Cooking time depends on the type of stock you're making. The longer you cook it for the more it will reduce and intensify. Meat stock usually takes around an hour and a half, whereas chicken stock can be made in forty-five minutes, and fish stock can take as little as half an hour.

7. Skim stock often. During the simmering process impurities will float to the surface and gather in a foamy scum. Have a spoon or a ladle handy and get that stuff out of there before it can cause any trouble.

8. Remove the layer of fat, because nobody likes greasy soup. The best way to do this is to let the stock cool and then scrape the fat layer away. If time is an issue, lay paper napkins on the stock's surface to soak it up.

9. Strain your stock when it comes off the stove. Pour it through a fine strainer or sieve to remove any impurities and chunks.

(Continued)

If you're concerned your strainer isn't fine enough, line it with cheesecloth.
10. When storing stock, cool it quickly and keep in the fridge for two to three days. Any longer than that, freeze it.

allowed to simmer, and will then require but fifteen minutes of gentle boiling. Salt should be added when the boiling commences, and this, for invalids in general, is the only seasoning required. When the extract is thus far prepared, it may be poured from the meat into a basin, and allowed to stand until any particles of fat on the surface can be skimmed off, and the sediment has subsided and left the soup quite clear, when it may be poured off gently, heated in a clean saucepan, and served. The scum should be well cleared as it accumulates.'

As straightforward as the recipe sounds, unfortunately it didn't work on a commercial scale. It took 30 kilograms of expensive European meat to produce just one kilogram of extract, making it far too costly to produce industrially. To overcome the problem Liebig opened a manufacturing plant named the Liebig Extract of Meat Company in Fray Bentos, Uruguay. Here he made use of cattle that in those days before widespread canning and freezing would otherwise have been killed for their hides alone. This savvy move reduced the cost of meat by a third. The cattle flesh was pulped using iron rollers and then soaked in hot water; the fat was then skimmed off from the liquid. Adding pressure and heat turned this soup into a thick, molasses-like concentration.

The company first marketed its product through physicians and apothecaries, who promoted its medicinal and nutritional virtues. 'Meat teas' made from Liebig's extract addressed 'all cases of weakness and digestive disorder' according to the company's advertising, and diminished 'brain-excitement' when served as a nightcap. Liebig never, it seems, shied away when it came to promoting the medical benefits of his invention. In an 1854 issue of his journal *Annalen der Chemie und*

Pharmacie he even claimed that meat tea could cure advanced typhus and inflamed ovaries.

The convenience of Liebig's product combined with his somewhat spurious health claims made it an immediate success, particularly with those in the medical establishment. After sampling one of the first jars of the manufactured extract in 1865, members of the Royal Medical and Chirurgical Society of London wrote that the 'whole medical profession owes a deep debt of gratitude to Liebig for having put into their hands a means of giving their patients the nutritive parts of animal food in a remarkably concentrated form'. By the late 1860s St Thomas' Hospital in London reported using twelve thousand pots of the stuff each year. It later became a staple in middle-class European households, and for soldiers and adventurers. It was even used by Sir Henry Morton Stanley on his trip to Africa.

But there was one gaping hole in Liebig's creation. As the product grew in popularity, disparaging chemists tested his extract and found that it contained very little in the way of fats and proteins, thus undermining its health-giving credentials. According to historian Mark Finlay, one experiment designed to uncover the extract's nutritional failings caused uproar at the time (and not for its casual animal cruelty). A German physiologist named Edward Kemmerich fed dogs a diet consisting solely of meat extract and shortly afterwards all of them died. When Kemmerich published the results of his experiment in 1868 he declared Liebig's extract poisonous. As the number of these attacks increased, Liebig changed tack, marketing the product not as a medicine but as a quick and easy way for overworked cooks to make a delicious meaty stew. The shrewd business move paid off and in 1899 an immensely popular version of Liebig extract aimed at home cooks was introduced – something we now know as Oxo. On a less meaty note, not content with creating what would become one of the world's most iconic brands Liebig went on to discover that brewer's yeast could be concentrated, bottled and eaten as a vegetarian alternative to meat extract. In 1902 the Marmite Food Company was founded in

Burton-on-Trent, Staffordshire, where the raw material was readily available from the town's many breweries. And we've never looked back.

The story doesn't end there. In 1870, during the Franco-Prussian War, Napoleon III ordered one million cans of beef to be sent to his troops. Large quantities of beef were available but the transport and storage of whole slabs of meat was too problematic. The conundrum was solved by a Scotsman living in Canada named John Lawson Johnston who invented Bovril, a dark-brown viscous meat glaze that could be turned into a warming, nourishing drink with the simple addition of hot water. Johnston created the extract by cooking beef trimmings at an extremely high temperature over a long period of time, which not only made the extract intensely rich but gave it a longer shelf life, too. The jewel in Bovril's crown, however, was its texture. All other meat extracts at the time were solid at room temperature owing to naturally occurring gelatin. Bovril was broken down into a semi-liquid thanks to a process known as chemical hydrolysis, making it easier to package, measure and use. For his services, Johnston was awarded the Order of the French Red Cross.

Reassuringly, the basic process used to make beef extract has remained largely unchanged since then. After a cow is slaughtered the most expensive bits of meat are sold off as premium cuts and steaks, while the cheaper more fiddly trimmings are used to create canned corned beef. To make the corned beef the trimmings are boiled, and the leftover meat-infused water (or 'beef juice' as they call it in the industry) is piped away into separate tanks. At this point you may be wondering where bones come into it. After all, it's the gelatin in bones that gives traditionally made beef stock its syrupy texture, right? In fact there are no bones in beef extract whatsoever. Instead the beef juice is boiled again and again over an eight-hour period until it has been reduced to a thick, salty, highly beefy concentrate. (During the process the extract is boiled so vigorously that any long-chain protein molecules are broken down into short chains, which has the effect of making it taste a lot more beefy. To put that a little more simply: when you tuck into a normal piece of unprocessed beef you only ever experience the beefy hit of a relatively small number of long-chain proteins. The more you smash these proteins up the more access your taste buds have to them.)

The downside, of course, is for the cows: it takes around one and a half whole specimens to make just one kilogram of meat extract. Think about that the next time you make gravy.

16

Do free-range eggs taste better?

GOING TO WORK ON an egg may be out of fashion, but as a nation we still find time to consume 30 million every single day. Eggs come from all sorts of breeds of hen, but whether your preference is for Columbian Blacktails, Burford Browns, Old Cotswold Legbars or just plain old own-brand essentials, they generally fall into two distinct categories: caged or free-range. As for which tastes best, that's a bit of a no-brainer, right? Just ask anyone who raises chickens, or anyone who's thinking about raising chickens, or anyone who gets eggs from anyone who raises chickens: fresh free-range eggs are brighter, firmer and tastier than anything from a cage.

Our faith in free-range is so strong that eggs produced by free-roaming birds now account for an impressive 50 per cent of all eggs sold in Britain; in the higher-value sector (i.e. the posher supermarkets) this number soars to a whopping 70 per cent. This may not sound that impressive to some but back in 1988 when junior health minister Edwina Currie declared that most of the country's egg production was infected with salmonella, free-range egg consumption accounted for less than 20 per cent of the entire market. And as if free-range eggs produced by others wasn't enough, some are even doing it themselves. The trend for keeping the planet's closest living evolutionary link to *Tyrannosaurus rex* in our back gardens began a few decades ago as a hobby among city- and suburbs-dwellers with large gardens and a penchant for re-enacting *The Good Life*. These days the trend has exploded into a fully fledged industry with pet shops and garden centres stocking chicken feed, poultry producers scrambling to keep up with the demand for birds, and dozens of manufacturers churning out hen coops in all manner of shapes and sizes. You can even buy fertilized eggs on eBay. The reason for this incredible surge in demand for backyard poultry? Not meat but the superior taste of super-fresh free-range eggs.

There's a strong element of distaste for battery farming in the mix too. If you've ever had the misfortune to see large-scale egg production in action, you'll easily understand why the general consensus is that eggs produced by caged chickens taste inferior. Although the barren battery cage, which barbarically squeezed each bird into an area the size of a piece of A4 paper, was banned in the EU in 2012, around 50 per cent of all eggs eaten in Britain are still produced by birds reared in 'colony cages'. Colony cages are essentially vast, sprawling sheds (some up to three storeys high) containing as many as a million chickens in each. Though a lot less crowded than your typical battery cage (space per hen is a luxurious 20 per cent larger than a piece of A4 paper) they are still restrictive, with hens unable to fly up to a perch to be safe from feather pecking and the litter area so small that effective 'dust bathing' (cleaning to you and me) often isn't possible. As a result hens can lose a large proportion of their feathers not just from damage caused by the sides of the cage but also by other hens – apparently frustrated by their lack of freedom.

Colony hens are bred to be highly productive and are kept at higher temperatures to increase egg output. A single chicken can produce as many as three hundred eggs a year (side note: chickens naturally live for six or more years but after twelve months of laying the hen's productivity will start to decline, so this is when most commercial laying hens are slaughtered). The good news for the consumer (but certainly not the chickens) is that eggs produced in this way can be around 50 per cent cheaper than eggs produced by free-range chickens, which by law have to be able to roam freely and express more of their natural behaviour, including stretching and flapping their wings, perching up high, foraging, scratching, dust bathing and laying their eggs in a comfortable nest.

Given the hugely differing experiences of colony and free-range chickens, you'd expect the quality of the latter's eggs to be very different – after all, it doesn't take Hugh Fearnley-Whittingstall to point out that the more stressed an animal is the worse it (or its produce) will taste. Yet study after study has shown that both the flavour and nutrition of eggs produced by caged and free-range birds are almost identical.

One of these studies, carried out in 2011 by poultry expert Dr Kenneth Anderson from North Carolina University, involved comparing the nutritional content of five hundred eggs produced by different methods over two years. The samples were collected on three occasions and sent to laboratories that analysed the eggs for levels of certain vitamins and fats. The study found that although the yolks of free-range eggs were generally a shade darker, they were not actually healthier. Levels of cholesterol, vitamin A (needed for healthy skin and bones) and vitamin E (essential for protecting the body's cells) were all the same. Writing in the *Journal of Poultry Science*, Dr Anderson concluded that 'a significant nutritional advantage of eggs produced by chickens housed on range versus in cages could not be established'.

The flavour of free-range eggs is also believed to be exactly the same as those produced by caged hens. In 2010 forty-four-year-old egg wholesaler Keith Owen pleaded guilty to passing off 100 million battery-farmed eggs as free-range or organic – many of them finding their way into Britain's biggest supermarkets including Sainsbury's, Morrisons and Tesco. Yet the battery eggs supplied by Owen were so similar in taste, flavour and texture to free-range eggs that not one person spotted the con. In fact nobody suspected a thing until murmurings began to circulate in the egg industry that there were far more British free-range and organic eggs being sold in shops than could possibly be laid in UK farms. Owen wasn't convicted of his crime until beady-eyed detectives inspected the eggs with a special ultraviolet light which showed the telltale marks of a cage that were completely invisible to the naked eye.

It is for good reasons that free-range eggs taste almost identical to those produced by caged hens. Humans have made chickens the most common and widespread bird on Earth; there are at least 50 billion of them worldwide and more than five hundred breeds. Yet almost all commercial eggs these days are produced by very similar hybrid chickens developed during the 1950s for their ability to lay large numbers of eggs. What's more, whether free-range or caged, these birds often have very similar diets, which is pretty much the only factor proven to markedly affect an egg's flavour. Other than organic chickens, which are generally fed on a diet of grass, plants, herbs, insects and organic grain, commercially reared free-range and caged chickens are mostly fed on generic, neutral-tasting chicken feed consisting of cereal, vegetable and animal proteins, with vitamin and mineral additives. As for those who believe they can tell the difference between a free-range and cage-reared egg simply by the colour of its yolk, look away now. While it is true that organic eggs are more likely to have a rich orange yolk (mainly on account of additional marigold in their diet) many caged hens have feed additives like marigold petal meal included in their diets anyway. And to add insult to injury, numerous studies have shown that the colour of an egg's yolk doesn't affect its flavour.

So what about those who swear that eggs produced in their own back garden are infinitely better than those from a colony cage? Well, they may just have a point – sort of. Though the flavour of an egg is only minimally affected by age, the texture of an egg's white and yolk will gradually get thinner over time. Mass-produced eggs are nearly always older than those bought straight from the farm, mainly because they have to be sorted, packaged and transported before they make it to the supermarket shelf. Ultimately this makes them harder to poach and more likely to spread when frying. Eggs straight out of the nest box boast tighter whites and taller-standing yolks mainly because they are so fresh. That's the real advantage in having chickens in your own backyard. As for flavour, free-range eggs might taste better simply because we perceive them to taste better. The egg industry has been conducting blind tasting tests for numerous years to help them develop ever more flavoursome eggs. During these studies subjects are never told how the chicken that produced the egg was reared, and the colour of the yolks is concealed with the help of clever lighting. And all because it is a recognized fact that humans perceive flavour based on pre-formed judgements.

Back in 1985 the Coca-Cola Company, in a bid to regain market share from Pepsi, decided to reformulate their flagship soft drink. They came up with a new formula that in blind tastings proved far more popular than both Pepsi and the original Coke. It seemed like a clear winner, and later that year they made a complete switch, discontinuing the original formula and marketing the new one as 'The New Taste of Coca-Cola'. The drink initially sold well, but Coca-Cola purists were not impressed and organizations were soon formed to petition the company to switch back, despite the fact that some of the organizers themselves had shown a preference for New Coca-Cola in the taste tests. More and more customers gave in to peer pressure as it became trendy to hate 'New Coke'. Three months later the company retreated and the original formula was reintroduced. New Coke was completely retired in 2002, despite the fact that the overwhelming majority of tasters preferred it. Such is the power of flavour perception.

If the flavour of eggs, like Coca-Cola, is largely a matter of perception then what incentive is left to pay the premium for 'better' eggs? Plenty. Rearing chickens in a free-range way is generally accepted by most to be a lot more humane than using colony cages – a form of farming that many argue is plagued with questionable ethics. Surely that alone is reason enough to go free-range. The fact that your mind tricks you into thinking these eggs taste better is just the icing on the cake.

Eggs: The Myths and Facts Unscrambled

1. All eggs contain salmonella.

Myth. Back in 1988, when Edwina Currie told us that most of the UK's eggs were infected with salmonella, she was partly right (many eggs were indeed infected). But her comments caused a 60 per cent drop in egg sales and she was forced to resign. Since then the industry has had a complete overhaul, particularly with the introduction of the Red Lion Quality Code of Practice in 1998, which includes the compulsory vaccination of egg-laying flocks against salmonella. With nearly 85 per cent of all UK eggs now carrying the Lion mark, the code is working. When salmonella peaked in 1993, over eighteen thousand cases of illness were recorded in the UK. By 2012 this had fallen to just 229, and not all of these cases can be blamed on eggs: watercress, bean sprouts and curry leaves are just some of the foods believed to be behind recent high-profile outbreaks. So it would seem that the risk of catching salmonella from British eggs is minuscule.

2. The egg came before the chicken.

Fact. According to research published in the *Journal of Palaeontology* in 2008, eggs came before chickens, because dinosaurs were forming bird-like nests and laying bird-like eggs long before birds (including chickens) evolved from dinosaurs.

3. Eggs clog up your arteries.

Myth. In the past there have been restrictions on the number of eggs people have been advised to eat in a week. This was because it was thought the amount of cholesterol in our bodies was directly caused by cholesterol in our food. Research has moved on, however, and we now know that much of the excess cholesterol in our bodies is actually produced by eating too much saturated fat. So while too many fried eggs and cheesy

(Continued)

omelettes may risk raising your cholesterol, it's actually the added fat from the frying or the addition of cheese (which is high in saturated fat) that's the problem. According to the British Heart Foundation, poached, boiled or scrambled eggs (without butter) are absolutely fine and there are no official restrictions on how many you should eat as part of a balanced diet. So, if you're worried about your cholesterol, cutting back on saturated fat will make more of an impact on your diet than cutting back on the number of eggs you eat.

4. Eggs can help to prevent blindness.

Fact. Eggs contain certain nutrients that are believed to protect your eyes against age-related macular degeneration (ARMD), a condition that accounts for around 50 per cent of all blindness and sight problems in the UK. The two nutrients lutein and zeaxanthin help to ward off the condition by allowing the eyes to filter harmful short-wavelength light and by curtailing other damaging effects on the macula, or the centre of the eye's retina. You can also boost your intake of lutein by eating leafy green vegetables like spinach, broccoli and kale.

5. You should always store eggs in the fridge.

Myth. There are two kinds of people in this world: those who put their eggs in the fridge and those who don't. Those in the pro-chill camp will tell you that a refrigerated egg will last longer and be less likely to spawn nasties such as *E. coli* and listeria. While there is a hint of truth in this – eggs in the fridge do generally keep for longer – there is no proof that refrigeration can prevent contamination from bacteria. Furthermore, though refrigerated eggs keep longer, some say their flavour deteriorates quicker. This is partly because an eggshell doesn't perfectly seal the contents from the outside world; it's actually full of millions of minuscule holes, which means an egg can absorb odours from other foods nearby, like half-onions, strong cheese and other smelly stuff you keep in the fridge.

17

Why is the cashew the only nut you cannot buy in its shell?

A BRIEF GLANCE AT GLOBAL nut consumption statistics and it's hard not to come to the conclusion that cashew nuts are the crack cocaine of the snack world, so addictive they should all carry the warning CAUTION: MAY BE HABIT FORMING. It turns out that global consumption of this beige, buttery-sweet nut has increased almost fourfold since 1987 and now stands at a staggering three million tons, making it by far the world's most popular nut. If that wasn't enough, production is expected to more than double in the next decade.

What was once a snack rarely found in specialist food shops let alone supermarkets is now the nibble of choice for Brits, from peckish pub-punters to health-conscious gourmands. Indeed so enchanted are we by the cashew nut's charm the Queen herself has taken them to heart. In 2013 it emerged that our monarch was allegedly so peeved that officers kept eating cashew nuts left out for guests at Buckingham Palace that an official memo was issued ordering them to 'keep their sticky fingers out'. And quite right too: at around £13 per kilogram cashew nuts are almost double the price of most other nuts – not that that's enough to stop us buying them. But have you ever stopped mid-gorge to ask yourself where they come from? Or, more specifically, why it is you can get almonds, walnuts, pistachios, brazil nuts, hazelnuts, peanuts, chestnuts, pecans and even macadamia nuts in their shells but never, ever cashews? The answer, it transpires, is more than a little ominous.

What probably doesn't come as a surprise to most is that cashews grow on the rather unimaginatively named cashew tree (or *Anacardium occidentale*, if you want to sound clever), a bushy, tropical evergreen that can reach a height of 35 feet and cover a space of up to 8,100 square feet. The tree is native to north-east Brazil but Portuguese missionaries introduced the species to Africa and South East Asia during the mid-sixteenth century in a deft attempt to stop soil erosion along the coast. The cashew flourished and these days you'll find them growing exten-sively throughout not just Brazil but Vietnam, India and Mozambique too, these four countries comprising the world's biggest cashew nut producers.

The cashew tree produces red flowers which in turn produce extremely juicy red and yellow pepper-like 'fruits' called cashew apples. Botanically speaking, cashew apples are not actually fruits at all, they're the swollen stalks of the true fruit of the cashew tree, a small kidney-shaped formation growing at the end of each apple known as a drupe. Chances are you've never tasted a cashew apple but these trop-ical, mango-like specimens are considered a delicacy throughout the regions where they grow and are used in all manner of ways. In the field, the fruits are picked by farmers and chewed for refreshment, the juice swallowed and the fibrous residue discarded. On a commercial scale they are preserved in syrup in glass jars and enjoyed as a sweet treat or distilled into an infamously strong (42 per cent) spirit called *fenny* (or *feni*). Sadly, the chances of your ever getting your hands on a cashew apple in Europe are slim to none, primarily because the 'fruit' is lumbered with an extremely fragile skin, rendering it inedible after long-haul transportation.

So, where does the cashew nut come into this? Well, a bit of a bomb-shell here: cashew nuts aren't actually nuts at all. Though classified as a nut in the culinary sense, the cashew is the seed found inside the kidney-shaped drupe of the cashew apple. The fruit might be delicious

Number Cruncher: Cashew Nuts

8,100 sq ft – area covered by the largest cashew nut tree in the world, located in Rio Grande do Norte, Brazil
3 million tons – amount of cashew nuts consumed every year
£1.5 billion – estimated worth of the global cashew nut trade
60 – percentage of all cashew nuts processed in India. The nut is among the country's top four agricultural exports, along with basmati rice, spices and tea.
3p – total amount earned in a day by some cashew nut processers in India
42 – percentage of alcohol found in the spirit made using the fermented juice of cashew apples

but woe betide anybody foolish enough to eat its seed. Every cashew nut is entombed in a thick double-layered shell containing an oil rich in something called urushiol, a resin chemically related to the toxin found in poison ivy. This clever substance works by tricking any human body it encounters into believing it is under attack. As soon as the immune system senses an attack it releases cell-damaging enzymes and toxins. The result is immensely itchy skin, a horrific burning sensation and, if ingested, potentially deadly inflammation of the lungs.

Fortunately, at some time pre-dating written history the people of Brazil figured out that if you want to sample the delights of the cashew nut you must remove the shell first. The challenge is doing this without getting urushiol all over your skin, eyes or mouth in the process. The answer, like the answer to so many of mankind's most baffling culinary conundrums, is of course fire – or, more precisely, heat. On a subsistence scale, cashew nut growers roast the raw nuts on sheets of metal over roaring open fires. As the nuts cook and expand their shells burst open like popcorn kernels. It sounds simple but the job is fraught with danger. When the nuts burst, fragments of shell are fired out like molten pieces of shrapnel, piercing and scalding the skin of anybody unlucky enough to be in the line of fire. More harmful is the thick cloud of toxic smoke that billows from the boiling oil. It's a fiddly, somewhat laborious method, but it works. After the last fragments of shell are roasted away the nuts are ready to scoff.

That's the traditional method for making cashew nuts safe, practised by small-scale farmers for millennia, but how are the thousands of cashew nuts we find in the supermarket today shelled? Every single one arrives at the factory in a raw state, meaning the toxic shell is well and truly intact. To remove the harmful oil the nuts are poured into huge industrial-scale boilers where heat and pressure force most of the oil out of the kernels. It is then piped away into storage tanks (more on this later).

Astonishingly, and controversially, the next part of the process relies entirely on manual labour: every single cashew nut you eat has been shelled by hand primarily because the job is far too delicate to be accomplished by machines. The problem is, though the majority of the oil has been removed at this stage, a small yet exceedingly caustic amount remains, which inevitably gets everywhere, including on the skin of those whose job it is to remove the shells. While in many factories rubber gloves are available not all workers can afford them, so many have to lather themselves in alkaline oil.

Unfortunately, the controversies surrounding the production of cashew nuts don't end there. In 2002 villagers in northern Kerala, India, won a short-term ban on the use of Endosulfan. The pesticide, sprayed over the country's cashew nut plantations, was blamed for causing severe mental disabilities and deformities among local children. Manufacturers of Endosulfan deny the connection, arguing that there is no scientific grounding to support the allegations. In 2011 a Human Rights Watch (HRW) report claimed that some forty thousand drug addicts detained in labour camps across Vietnam were being forced to produce the country's cashew nuts. The recovering heroin addicts, according to the report, spent six to ten hours a day husking and skinning nuts, suffering painful burns as a result. Finally, in 2013 the cashew nut found itself at the centre of another controversy, after accusations that Western retailers were reaping unfairly large profits, leaving farmers and processers with a pittance. Campaigners claimed some supermarkets earn over £1 from a bag of cashews sold for £2.50, while the factory worker who sits all day cracking open the harmful shells makes just 3p.

It isn't all bad news though. The cashew tree, blamed for so much suffering over the last decade or so, has long been exploited in folk medicine for its supposed health-giving properties. Though harmful in large enough quantities, the oil is believed by many in cashew-nut-growing communities to aid recovery from a hotchpotch of different illnesses and conditions including ulcers, cracked feet, gingivitis, dysentery, fever, piles, hyperglycaemia and malaria. In Brazil the old leaves of cashew trees are applied to the skin to heal burns, and in Africa the bark is used to treat sore gums, toothache, diarrhoea and thrush. Finally, in India farmers use the bark to make herbal tea – a beverage said to aid the treatment of asthma, common colds and congestion, and even the bite of a venomous snake. Not bad going for a single species of tree.

It might sound like a load of old baloney to some but doctors in the West are beginning to make use of the humble cashew too. The caustic oil piped away at the beginning of the shelling process contains a substance known as anacardic acid, which has been found to have antibiotic qualities. In fact this acid is so effective a number of high-profile medical studies have found it capable of killing certain strains of MRSA and tuberculosis. Some even believe it has the revolutionary potential to inhibit the growth of certain cancerous tumours. The catch? Extracting medical-grade anacardic acid is a highly complicated, energy-intensive process that therefore comes with an extremely hefty price tag. A single gram (roughly the weight of a cashew nut) can set you back as much as £12,000 – roughly three hundred times the cost of crack cocaine.

Cashews in a Nutshell

The tree: The cashew tree (*Anacardium occidentale*) is a tropical evergreen plant native to north-east Brazil. However, between 1560 and 1565 Portuguese missionaries introduced the species to Goa. From there it spread throughout South East Asia and eventually to Africa.

The fruit (that isn't a fruit): The cashew tree produces red flowers which in turn produce the red and yellow pepper-like cashew apples – which aren't actually fruits at all. The real fruit of the cashew tree is the small kidney-shaped drupe growing at the end of each apple. In cashew-nut-growing countries a drink is commonly made from these apples that's famed for its mango-like flavour. In Goa the apple juice is fermented and double-distilled to create the strong alcoholic beverage *fenny* (or *feni*).

The nut (that isn't a nut): Each drupe contains a single cashew nut which, though classified as a nut in the culinary sense, is actually a seed.

The de-shelling process: The traditional way is to roast the nuts over an open fire – a hazardous task because the shells burst and fire off red-hot toxic fragments, and the oil within the shells gives off dangerous fumes. The commercial method aims to dissipate these poisonous properties using roasting cylinders, though the inner shells must still be broken open by hand and the kernels heated to remove the skins.

18

Is it OK to eat mouldy bread?

THERE'S SOMETHING DEEPLY INTIMIDATING about the microscopic fungi we call mould. And with good reason. It is one of the most successful and ubiquitous forms of life on the planet, with millions of invisible spores surrounding us at any given time, many of which are capable of surviving the types of conditions that would make most bacteria curl up and die. Worse still, given half a chance mould will spread its twine-like fingers through almost any of our hard-earned food, be it fruit, vegetables, cheese, meat, jam or the thing it seems to crave most: bread. Left to its own devices it will reduce all to a squidgy, inedible mess of incandescent coloured splodges and wispy white fur.

But how harmful is the type of mould we typically find on a slice of bread? Opinions, as you may expect, are well and truly divided. Some won't touch a piece of mouldy bread with a bargepole, declaring it a harbourer of bad bacteria and a harbinger of serious ill health. The only answer for people with such views is to consign the affected slice or loaf to the bin. Others take a more pragmatic approach, bravely cutting away the offending part and toasting the bread in the belief that this will make it safe. A select group, mainly comprising the hard and the thrifty, simply don't give a monkey's and will stubbornly chomp their way through a slice of mighty white whatever the degree of infection.

Though we tend to tarnish all moulds with the same brush, the truth is there are thousands upon thousands of known species of mould, many of which we consume on a daily basis without even knowing it. Some of these are not only perfectly safe to eat or ingest but are actively encouraged by food producers because of their flavour-giving properties. Kōji moulds, for example, have been cultured on grains of steamed rice in eastern Asia for many centuries, where they are used to break down the starch in rice, barley and sweet potatoes, and in a process known as saccharification during the production of sake. The same mould is also used to ferment a soybean and wheat mixture to make soy sauce (something most of us, including those who wouldn't go near a slice of mouldy bread, have tried at least once).

Another mould, *Botrytis cinerea*, is an essential ingredient in some of the world's finest dessert wines such as Sauternes and Trockenbeerenauslese (ten out of ten if you can pronounce that one). The producers of these wines deliberately spray *Botrytis* spores over their vineyards, exposing the vines to the attractive-sounding infection 'noble rot', which after a short while causes the grapes to dehydrate, making them partially 'raisinized'. The resulting wine is celebrated the world over for its exquisite sweetness, which experts say is reminiscent of caramel, honey and apricot. Some of the world's best meats rely on mould, too. The process of dry-ageing ham and beef often promotes the growth of certain moulds such as the genus *Thamnidium* on the meat's surface, which is trimmed off before the meat is prepared for cooking. Far from being a problem, these moulds actually complement the natural enzymes in the meat, helping to tenderize and concentrate its flavour.

One of the most famous moulds is *Penicillium*, the mould that gave the world penicillin, an antibiotic that some estimate has saved the lives of 200 million people since its discovery by Scottish scientist Alexander Fleming in 1928. Its lesser-known siblings are good friends to the food industry. Some of the best salami manufacturers on the continent infect their sausages with the powdery white mould *Penicillium nalgiovensis* to improve depth of flavour and reduce spoilage during curing, and *Penicillium camemberti* is sprayed on to Camembert and Brie to help create their characteristic white rinds and soft texture. The mould that gives blue cheeses such as Stilton, Gorgonzola and Roquefort their trademark tangy, salty flavour and rich, creamy texture is *Penicillium roqueforti*, a mould found in the soil of caves in the French village of Roquefort.

The use of moulds like these in the production of food is testament to the fact that not all strains are dangerous. Indeed some moulds are believed by some to be highly beneficial to our health. Red yeast rice, a common ingredient in Asian cooking derived from the mould *Monascus purpureus*, has been used in Chinese medicine for centuries to improve circulation and ease digestive problems. Some recent medical studies have found the yeast to contain chemicals that work much like prescription statins, lowering 'bad' LDL cholesterol. In 2012 a group of doctors at a Cambridge-based biotech company published a report hypothesizing that mouldy cheeses like Roquefort have anti-inflammatory properties and as a result may help to improve cardiovascular health. According to the authors of the report, the anti-inflammatory proper-ties of blue cheese may be one of the reasons French people have one of the longest life expectancies in Europe, despite indulging in a diet high in saturated fat. It should probably be pointed out here that the doctors in question have no proof that mouldy cheese can make you live longer. So probably best not to go straight out and buy Waitrose's entire stock of Roquefort.

Does all of this mean we should be more relaxed about the kind of mould we find on out-of-date food? Er, no, not really. The US Department of Agriculture suggests that hard cheese and vegetables such as carrots, potatoes and squashes can be salvaged by cutting out at least an inch around the affected area, but they also stipulate that any-thing else found to be harbouring mould should be instantly chucked in the bin, including soft fruits and vegetables, hot dogs, cooked meat, casseroles, pasta, soft cheese, yoghurt, sour cream, jelly, peanut butter, legumes and nuts. Think that sounds a little OTT? The UK Food Standards Agency is even stricter, suggesting that the safest option is to throw all mouldy food away, whether it's hard cheese or not. Too

Breaking the Mould: Five Foods that have Learned to Love the Blue Stuff

While many of us wouldn't touch mould with a barge pole, some of our favourite foods are in fact derived from it.

Sake: In order to brew beer, barley goes through a malting process during which enzymes within the barley convert starch molecules into sugars. The fundamental difference between sake and beer is that sake rice does not contain the kinds of enzymes that barley does, so an additional ingredient is needed – a strain of mould known as Kōji-kin (or, if you want to sound scientific, *Aspergillus oryzae*). The mould is delicately distributed over steamed sake rice in a humid room and left to grow over a period of forty-eight to seventy-two hours until all the grains of rice are coated in a furry white layer of mould. Only then is the rice ready to be fermented into sake.

Dessert wine: Some of the most acclaimed dessert wines in the world are made with the help of 'noble rot' (*Botrytis cinerea*). This mould has a bad reputation among farmers for causing considerable damage to soft fruits like tomatoes and strawberries but in the right environment it can actually improve certain varieties of grape. It does this by decreasing the grape's water content, leaving behind a higher percentage of solids such as sugars, fruit acids and minerals.

Aged beef: Many chefs agree that dry-ageing – hanging a side of beef in a humidity-controlled cooler for up to three weeks – is essential for a great-tasting steak. As the meat hangs, dehydration concentrates the flavour into a rich, pungent beefy taste and enzymes within the beef start to break down the connective tissues, making it more tender. The process also promotes the growth of certain moulds such as *Thamnidium*, which instead of causing the meat to go rotten actually aid the work of the enzymes.

(Continued)

Roquefort: Named after the village of Roquefort in Aveyron, in the south of France, this blue cheese is famous for its pungent smell, tangy flavour and rich, creamy texture – and it's all thanks to a mould known as *Penicillium roqueforti* found in the soil of local caves. Traditional cheese makers create the mould by leaving bread to rot in these caves for six to eight weeks until nothing is left but a crusty outer shell and a furry blue interior. The mould is then dried to produce a powder, inserted into giant saltshakers and scattered over fresh curds, effectively planting the seeds of the blue mould. Once enough *P. roqueforti* is in the cheese, it is wrapped up and left to mature for another ten months.

Quorn: This vegetarian alternative to meat is made from a fungal protein called mycoprotein, which in turn is derived from a microfungi known as *Fusarium venenatum*. The mould is grown in continually oxygenated water in large, sterile fermentation tanks and fed glucose syrup. When the desired amount of mycoprotein has been created it is drawn off from a tap at the bottom of the fermenter before being separated and purified.

cautious? Well, while certain moulds, usually those created in controlled conditions, are harmless to our health – even beneficial – others can cause allergic reactions and aggravate respiratory conditions (particularly if you suffer from asthma). Some moulds, under warm and humid conditions, can even produce highly toxic substances called mycotoxins, a group of naturally occurring chemicals found to cause all manner of health problems including kidney damage, gastrointestinal disturbances, reproductive disorders, suppression of the immune system and liver cancer.

So where does this leave bread? A single slice of bread left to fester for three weeks or so will typically develop as many as ten different strains of mould. The good news is that the majority of these are benign, meaning you could consume them with no adverse effect on your health. In fact the green spores of mould you often find forming on the crust of gone-off bread are most often a strain of *Penicillium* (i.e. very closely related to the kind of mould you find on Roquefort cheese). The bad news is that some bread, usually the extremely rotten variety, can contain toxic strains of mould which look dangerously similar but can in fact be deadly. One of these is a yellow-green mould called *Aspergillus flavus* which produces aflatoxin – one of the most poisonous substances known to man. The scariest thing about this strain of mould is it's actually pretty common; if you were to leave a slice of bread out in the open long enough it's likely it would make an unwelcome appearance. No matter how clean your kitchen is. And that's why it's never a good idea to eat a slice of mouldy bread.

Bin It or Trim It: A Brief Guide to Eating Mouldy Food

While a dusting of white mould on the surface of food, no matter how benign its appearance, is never 100 per cent safe, with a little bit of caution it can often be removed safely. Other moulds, however, can be a lot more dangerous.

Hard cheese: Keep it. If only a small amount of white powdery mould has formed on hard cheese it's generally fine to keep. A good rule of thumb is to remove about an inch of cheese around the affected area before consuming. Just be sure to keep your knife out of the mould to avoid cross-contamination and always rewrap the cheese in a fresh covering afterwards.

Nuts and peanut butter: Throw them. Mouldy nuts can contain aflatoxin, which has been linked to liver cancer.

Hard salami and dry-cured ham: Keep it. Salami and some dry-cured hams are often covered in a fine layer of white

(Continued)

mould. This kind is more often than not completely benign and is almost always introduced by the manufacturer to aid the development of flavour. However, if you spot anything more than a dusting of white mould, chuck it.

Blue cheese: It depends. The blue veins in cheeses like Roquefort, Gorgonzola and Stilton are vital in terms of giving the cheeses their distinctive creamy texture and zingy, salty flavour. But again, if you spot any other strains of mould you don't recognize (particularly if they're not blue) it's always best to err on the side of caution and throw it in the bin.

Yoghurt and sour cream: Throw them. Mould and bacteria find it difficult to penetrate hard cheeses, allowing you to trim off the affected area. But with a soft food like yoghurt, mould and bacteria can accumulate throughout the product, meaning not all the harmful bacteria will be visible. Apart from ruining the taste of your yoghurt, these moulds can cause numerous health problems if ingested, including allergic reactions and respiratory complications.

Firm fruits and veggies: Keep them. A tough vegetable like a carrot can have a small amount of white mould on its surface but still be perfectly edible, mainly because the mould has trouble penetrating deep into the food. Trim off about an inch around the mould before consuming.

Soft fruits: Throw them. Very soft fruits like raspberries and strawberries are clearly inedible when mouldy, but even soft fruits with thick rinds such as oranges are easily affected by mould. Unfortunately, the tough rind doesn't offer much protection, meaning mould can permeate the skin and spread quickly through the fleshy interior.

19

Do the bubbles in champagne really go to your head?

CHAMPAGNE HAS LONG BEEN considered a form of liquid gold, a decadent drink for the most special occasions. But it has a darker side. How many people have you heard say that champagne goes straight to their head, making them feel giggly, giddy, even out of control? The answer is probably quite a lot. In fact chances are you've probably experienced the dizzying effects of fizz yourself. As for the cause of such potent inebriation, ask any armchair scientist worth their salt and they'll blame it on the bubbles. 'They force the alcohol into your bloodstream,' say some. 'It isn't the alcohol that gets you drunk,' say others, 'it's the specific type of gas found in champagne bubbles.' If it is the bubbles themselves that make you drunk, then what are champagne producers putting in their wine that could possibly make us feel so out of control?

Bubbles have been occurring spontaneously in still wine since time immemorial. And the tendency for still wine from the Champagne region to sparkle lightly was noted as far back as the Middle Ages. The trouble was, nobody could work out where the bubbles were coming from and as a result they were attributed to all manner of unusual phenomena from the changing phases of the moon to the presence of evil spirits. Whatever the cause, until the seventeenth century this naturally occurring fizz was actually considered a fault in wine rather than a virtue. So much so that the godfather of champagne, Benedictine monk Dom Pérignon, was actually chastised by his elders for being unable to create a completely bubble-free wine. It wasn't that people didn't like the fizz – writers from the Ancient Greeks onwards have extolled the flavour-enhancing qualities of bubbles – it was because it made wine making a hazardous job: as the number of bubbles increases in a bottle of wine so too does its propensity to explode.

Though nobody knew it at the time, the bubbles found in sparkling wine were not the result of mischievous spirits, or indeed the waxing and waning moon, but of something known as secondary fermentation. During the cold winters in the Champagne region temperatures would drop so low that the fermentation process (whereby sugars are con-verted into alcohol by yeast) was prematurely halted, leaving some residual sugar and dormant yeast. If the wine was bottled in this state, it became a time bomb. When the weather warmed in the spring, the yeast roused itself and began generating carbon dioxide that would at best push the cork out of the bottle, and at worst explode it, starting a chain reaction: nearby bottles, also under pressure, would break from the shock of the first breakage, and so on. It was hazardous for employees and injurious to that year's production.

Amazingly, it was actually the Brits who managed to harness cham-pagne's explosive power. When the wine was shipped to England, where it had become exceedingly fashionable following the arrival of Epicurean Charles de Saint-Évremond in the mid-seventeenth century, it was housed in glass bottles made in pioneering coal-fuelled ovens which were far more durable than the bottles being produced by French wood-fired furnaces. Furthermore the English had also rediscovered the use of hardy cork stoppers, once used by the Romans but forgotten for centuries. These two innovations meant that champagne served in England always underwent some form of secondary fermentation without any exploding bottles. Thus from the mid-1600s onwards champagne in England was served sparkling, unlike in France where it was generally always flat.

Intrigued by this newfangled fashionable wine, the English tried to get to the bottom of what made it sparkle. In 1662 the English scientist Christopher Merret hit the jackpot and presented a paper detailing how the presence of sugar in a wine was what made it fizzy, and that nearly any wine could be made to sparkle by adding sugar to it before bottling. As a result of this revelation British wine merchants were able to fine-tune the carbonation of sparkling champagne long before the French. Indeed the process of secondary fermentation, as documented by Merret, is still in use by champagne makers today. Like any other wine, grapes (usually Pinot Noir, Chardonnay and Pinot Meunier) are crushed and their juices fermented. Unlike your average bottle of plonk a small amount (several grams or so) of yeast and sugar is placed into each bottle before sealing it. The bottles are left to condition for a minimum of one and a half years. During this time the additional yeast converts the sugar into alcohol and in doing so creates carbon dioxide, thus giving the wine its trademark fizz. *Et voilà.*

Well, not quite. Not content with the natural bubbles produced by secondary fermentation humans invented the champagne flute, a glass that is exceedingly good at both creating and retaining champagne's trademark fizz. Remarkably, bubbles won't form unless they've got a starting point, which in the case of a glass is its roughest or dirtiest point. If there are any specks of dust or fibre inside the glass you'll see a stream of bubbles coming from that point, and that's why it's always important to polish your wine glasses. Many champagne flutes (particularly those at the more expensive end of the spectrum) come equipped with a small cross etched at the bottom of the glass which encourages the bubbles to start at the bottom and work their way upwards.

So why all this effort just to make more bubbles? Well, bubbles, it turns out, are not just pretty, innocuous novelties designed to entertain you as you stare blankly into your glass. No, bubbles are crucial to the whole sensory experience of champagne. If you've ever left a half-finished bottle of champagne in the fridge for too long and then tasted it flat you'll understand that without its effervescence all its most important elements – its flavours, aromas and, of course, that gentle fizz across the tongue – are completely lost. This is because as bubbles rise they drag liquid up with them to the top of the glass, and that liquid then has to travel back down the sides. This in effect creates an underwater fountain, continually churning the champagne and keeping its flavour molecules in suspension.

Many of these aromatic flavour molecules stick to the rising bubbles and so are delivered directly to the surface of the drink. Research has shown there are up to thirty times more flavour-enhancing chemicals in these bubbles than in the rest of the drink. When the bubbles pop they spit tiny droplets upwards; a single burst bubble can project a flavour molecule an astounding ten centimetres into the air. The best bit? Due to the small, focused opening of a champagne flute many of these flavour molecules are fired straight up the nose, giving you a big hit of flavour before you've even taken a sip.

And just when you thought bubbles couldn't get any better, a recent study has found that the human tongue can actually taste the carbon dioxide itself. Previous research had concluded that the tingling sensation produced by fizzy drinks was due to the bursting of carbon dioxide bubbles, but a publication in the journal *Science* in 2009 reported that taste receptors on the tongue which detect the flavour of sour food also respond to the gases of carbonated drinks, which may explain why the bursting of champagne bubbles on the tongue is so pleasurable.

So bubbles clearly improve the flavour of champagne, but can they actually make you drunk? The general assumption throughout history has been that it is the social situation in which champagne is drunk and not its bubbles that makes one squiffy. It would certainly make sense: we tend to consume champagne, often on empty stomachs, when celebrating something or at events where it is free-flowing (weddings, openings, office parties, birthdays). When alcohol is free and you're in the mood to celebrate, the chances are you'll consume a lot of it. However, in 2001 scientist Dr Fran Ridout from the University of Surrey blew this theory out of the water. In a study aimed at understanding the intoxicating effects of bubbles, Ridout threw a couple of 'drinks parties' for volunteers in her department. She gave champagne to twelve volunteers, half of which drank fizzy champagne while the other half had flat champagne, purged of its bubbles beforehand with a whisk. The following week she repeated the experiment but gave each volunteer the opposite kind of champagne – that way everyone tried both types of wine. Ridout also adjusted the intakes so that everyone drank exactly the same amount of alcohol per kilogram of body mass.

Alcohol levels rose much faster among the bubbly drinkers. After just five minutes they had an average of 0.54 milligrams of alcohol per millilitre of blood, whereas those drinking flat champagne averaged just 0.39 milligrams. The bubbles in the champagne also seemed to have an impact on the subjects' perception. During tests carried out to measure their reaction times, bubbly-drinkers took 200 milliseconds longer on average to respond than when they were sober. Those on flat wine took only an extra 50 milliseconds.

If this study does indeed provide conclusive evidence that bubbly alcohol can make you drunker than still alcohol, how exactly it works remains something of a mystery. One theory is that bubbles actually encourage the body to soak up more alcohol. In order to get you drunk, alcohol has to enter your bloodstream and the only way it can do this is through your digestive system. About 20 per cent enters through the stomach while the other 80 per cent enters through the small intestine. What controls the passage of alcohol from the stomach to the small intestine is a tiny valve called the pyloric sphincter, which has to open to allow the alcohol through. According to Ridout, the bubbles in champagne stimulate the valve to open, allowing alcohol to pass through to the small intestines and into the bloodstream more easily.

However, if you're one of those people who find champagne a little too intoxicating then don't go wielding the whisk just yet. Ridout's experiment showed that bubbles can only momentarily increase alcohol absorption; the difference in blood alcohol levels between those drinking the bubbly and those drinking the flat champagne reduced significantly about thirty-five minutes after consumption. What's more, research has emerged recently that challenges the assertion that bubbles can make you drunker. In 2007 a team of scientists from the University of Manchester performed a similar experiment to Ridout's, but instead of champagne, a group of volunteers were given vodka mixed with either still or carbonated water. Adding the gaseous mixer bumped up the initial rate of alcohol absorption into the blood by around 50 per cent on average. But this rate varied wildly among the volunteers. In fact three of the twenty-one volunteers absorbed the bubbly cocktail more slowly than the flat one, and for four subjects the carbonation made no difference at all.

So while carbonation might initially increase the rate at which alcohol is absorbed into the blood (though there is no guarantee it will), the heightened effect is temporary. After half an hour or so you're going to feel essentially the same as if you had knocked back a glass of bubbleless Chardonnay.

The best way to stop the bubbles from going to your head in the first place? There's no question that food delays the emptying of the stomach contents into the small intestine. So pre-drink nibbles or a full-blown meal are a surefire way to slow down inebriation. Failing that, there's always the old adage that everything should be enjoyed in moderation. Yeah right . . .

Champagne: Myths Debunked

1. Placing a spoon in the neck of a bottle of champagne will prevent it from losing its fizz.

False. Unfortunately numerous studies have proved this to be nothing more than an old wives' tale. The truth is, once a bottle of champagne has been opened it will continue to lose carbon dioxide and there's nothing you can do to stop it. The good news is it's easy to slow down the rate at which the bubbles are lost. All you need to do is keep the bottle cold. Carbon dioxide is more soluble at low temperatures so cold liquids better retain their dissolved gas. Some sparkling wines are so saturated with carbon dioxide they can remain bubbly in the fridge for days.

2. The bigger the bottle the better the flavour.

Yes, it is true what they say: size really does matter. Sales of champagne stored in 1.5-litre magnums have risen by around 60 per cent over the past few years. It's a trend that goes all the way from supermarket own-label brands to the decadent heights of Dom Pérignon. The reason? Though the volume of a magnum is bigger than that of a normal bottle, the size of the neck remains the same, meaning only a comparatively small amount of the entire volume of wine is in contact with the air between its surface and the cork, slowing down the flavour-ruining effects of oxidation.

3. Vintage champagnes generally taste better.

True. Generally speaking, when it comes to flavour vintage champagnes always have the upper hand. This is because they are made from one exceptional harvest of grapes from a single year rather than a blend (cuvée) from several harvest years. Additionally, vintage champagnes have to be aged for at least

(Continued)

seven years in cellars before release, and any length of time you age a wine it softens the edges and creates a smoother taste. What's more, in years when the vintage is inconsistent, non-vintage champagnes are made, using wines from three to five vintages to create consistency in taste.

4. Champagne should be served on ice.

False. As everybody knows, champagne is a drink best served chilled. The best way to do this is either in the fridge or in an ice bucket (something invented at a time when people didn't have refrigeration). However, once chilled, champagne doesn't then need to be kept on ice unless you plan to drink it over the course of several hours. If the champagne gets too cold its taste and aroma will be dulled.

20

Where do the bacteria in probiotic yoghurt come from, and are they actually any good for you?

IT'S HARD TO IMAGINE but there was in fact a time when the words 'pro-biotic' and 'good bacteria' meant absolutely nothing to the vast majority of the Great British public. Then in the early 1990s something called Yakult arrived on our shores: a thimble-sized portion of floodwater-brown liquid that sold itself as a fermented milk drink with an added strain of healthy bacteria called *Lactobacillus casei Shirota* (not that anybody could pronounce it). 'But why would I want to drink bacteria?' we said to ourselves. 'It's bad for you.' But of course it didn't matter what logic told us. Wooed by the brand's utilitarian design, medical-sounding terminology and cute pocket-sized packaging we threw caution to the wind and began to buy the stuff by the lorry load.

Fast-forward a couple of decades and there are literally hundreds of probiotic products on the market all made using a variety of strains of 'good bacteria' and claiming to help in the fight against a litany of ail-ments including high cholesterol, constipation, obesity, diarrhoea, gut infections and common colds. And consumers, it seems, have been lap-ping it up. Some estimates suggest that around 60 per cent of UK households regularly use probiotic yoghurts, while the UK industry alone is worth a massive £200 million a year. But how many of us really know what 'good bacteria' are or what they do to our body? And have you ever stopped to think where the bacteria come from?

Probiotics are, quite simply, micro-organisms that some say provide health benefits when consumed. The term itself is relatively new – mysteriously nobody seems to know the exact origin of the word but many believe it was coined by German food scientist Werner Kollath in 1953 when he defined 'probiotika' (Latin for 'pro-life') as 'active substances that are essential for a healthy development of life' – but probiotics have in fact been enjoyed for many thousands of years in the form of fermented foods. Prior to refrigeration and pasteurization, fermentation allowed food to be stored and preserved for later use, preventing spoilage through the natural defences of lactic acid-producing bacteria. But it wasn't until the early twentieth century that humans began to understand the positive role played by this kind of bacteria.

Often credited as the 'inventor' of probiotics is Russian scientist and Nobel laureate Élie Metchnikoff, who first suggested it would be possible to replace harmful microbes in the gut with useful microbes. Metchnikoff had observed that certain rural populations in Europe, for example in Bulgaria and Russia, who lived largely on milk fermented by lactic acid bacteria lived exceptionally long lives for the time. Based on this, Metchnikoff proposed that consumption of fermented milk would 'seed' the intestine with harmless lactic acid bacteria and suppress the growth of infections. Metchnikoff himself began consuming this sour milk and found his health did indeed improve. Friends and colleagues soon followed his example, and physicians began prescribing the sour-milk diet for their patients.

After Metchnikoff's death in 1916 scientists began to propose that bacteria originating in the human gut were likely to be more effective than those sourced from milk, and in 1935 certain strains of a bacteria called *Lactobacillus acidophilus* were found to be very active when implanted in the digestive system of a human. More experiments were carried out using the bacteria and encouraging results were found, especially when it came to treating chronic constipation.

In the Know: Foods Naturally High in Probiotics

Probiotic yoghurts may have enjoyed a meteoric rise in popularity over the last twenty years or so but they certainly aren't the only foods to contain 'good bacteria'.

Kombucha tea (fermented tea): A lightly sparkling black tea mainly drunk in China and Korea. Unlike other teas kombucha is fermented with bacteria and yeast not only making it slightly fizzy but probiotic, too.

Miso soup: Miso is a culinary staple in Japanese culture, made by fermenting soybeans with barley or brown rice and mixing them with salt and fungus. The final product is then made into a paste and used in soups, salad dressings and sauces.

Yoghurt: The bacteria traditionally used to make yoghurt are also responsible for many of yoghurt's supposed benefits such as improved intestinal health and increased immune function. Just make sure the yoghurt you buy contains live, active cultures.

Kefir: A sweet, tarty and slightly carbonated milk drink made by fermenting cow, goat or sheep milk with yeast and certain species of bacteria. The fermented liquid is not only rich in probiotics but also high in vitamins A, B and D.

Pickled cabbage: Probiotic yoghurts usually contain only one strain of bacteria. Raw sauerkraut and its spicier Asian cousin kimchi have been found to contain over thirteen different species of gut-friendly bacteria.

Olives: As a result of fermentation, some traditionally brined olives, like the Spanish Gordal variety, can have as many as 100 billion *lactobacilli* (friendly bacteria) residing on their surface.

There are numerous reasons why modern humans appear to be suffering from a dearth of good bacteria, one of which is our diet. While traditionally fermented foods like miso, kimchi, sauerkraut, kombucha tea and, of course, good old-fashioned yoghurt continue to be eaten, modern food-processing methods such as pasteurization, refrigeration, refining and factory processing have drastically limited their availability. The result? A huge reduction in the number of naturally occurring enzymes, bacteria and yeasts in our diet. It also doesn't help that most of us regularly use antibacterial products and consume meat, poultry and dairy products treated with antibiotics.

And there are a number of other things that can throw our levels of good bacteria out of balance. One of these is stress. For a study carried out in 2006 a group of genetically identical rats living in the same controlled environment and eating the same standardized food were split into two groups. One group was left alone while the other was regularly stressed (by being placed on a small platform surrounded by water, in case you were wondering – rats hate swimming apparently). Examination of the stressed rats' poo (somebody's got to do it) showed that harmful bacteria had latched on to cells in the intestinal wall and nearby lymph nodes – which suggests stress alone is enough to upset your gut's bacterial balance. Other things believed to decimate your body's number of natural bacteria include antibiotics, C-section births, bottle feeding, early introduction of food, a low-fibre diet (i.e. not enough fruit and veg) and poor digestion.

But who cares if our levels of good bacteria are a little out of whack? The human gastrointestinal tract, including the mouth, oesophagus, stomach and intestines, is home to around 100 trillion – yes, trillion – bacteria happily living inside us, essentially rendering us giant walking, talking bacteria colonies. To put this into perspective: we have so much bacteria inside us it accounts for around 3kg of our total weight (and up to half the weight of our poo). Indeed if a visitor from another planet were to analyse all the cells that make up your body he/she/it would have to come to the conclusion that you were only 10 per cent human because 90 per cent of the living cells in your body are bacteria. When you consider that, it should come as no surprise that keeping them in good order is paramount to our health. This is particularly true of the bacteria found in the gastrointestinal tract (collectively known as microflora), which have been found to help us digest food, protect us from pathogens (harmful micro-organisms), produce vitamins and other nutrients, keep our guts healthy, and maintain our immune system. The job of probiotics, then, is to try to boost the numbers of good bacteria in our gut, thus defending us against illnesses and infections caused by harmful bacteria.

But hold on, don't go raiding the shelves of your nearest supermarket just yet. Though the health benefits of 'good bacteria' are well known the effectiveness of probiotic supplements (such as yoghurts) in terms of delivering them remains widely contested. One of the most common criticisms levelled at probiotics by experts is that they simply aren't robust enough to have any effect on your gut; there may be as many as a billion bacteria in a single pot of yoghurt but that's small change in comparison to the 100 trillion in your digestive system. Furthermore, of those billion bacteria it is debatable how many actually make it to the lower gut.

Such criticisms are taken so seriously that the World Health Organization's definition of probiotics as 'live micro-organisms which when administered in adequate amounts confer a health benefit on the host' is not accepted by the European Food Safety Authority (EFSA), which argues that the definition embeds a health claim that is not measurable. Indeed in 2010 EFSA rejected 180 such claims by probiotic brands – 'maintains digestive comfort', 'boosts defences' and the like – on the basis that there simply wasn't enough evidence to support them. That same year EFSA examined twelve studies submitted by Yakult for its own strain of probiotic bacteria, *Lactobacillus casei Shirota*, and found that all were inadequate to support the company's claim that its products maintained immune defences against the common cold. Yakult's appeal request in 2011 was denied by EFSA.

The effectiveness of probiotic supplements, then, is open to debate. But what about the ingredients used in them – are they what they claim to be? You'll be glad to know that probiotic yoghurts do indeed contain lots of 'good bacteria', which are combined with the yoghurt during production. As for where these bacteria come from . . . probiotic fans may wish to look away now. Though some strains of bacteria come from fermented plant matter, much of the bacteria found in probiotics are actually derived from humans. One of Europe's largest manufacturers is Finnish company Valio which makes probiotic yoghurt for hundreds of brands around the globe. They rely on a strain of bacteria called *Lactobacillus rhamnosus*, which they've trademarked with the snappier name LGG. The bacteria was discovered in 1983 when it was isolated from the faeces of a healthy American. Since then laboratories have been reproducing LGG endlessly from just this one original sample, and it is one of the most widely consumed probiotics in the world. The good news is you aren't consuming a tiny piece of Stateside poo every time you down a shot of probiotic yoghurt, it's the bacteria isolated from the poo – a very big difference.

Five Things You Probably Never Knew About Probiotics

1. We get our first probiotics during birth.

When a baby is born it receives its first dose of a probiotic known as *Bifidus infantis*, a form of bacteria found in healthy birth canals to fend off infection. This is one of the reasons it is considered so important for mothers to optimize their friendly bacteria levels before giving birth. After birth, consumption of breast milk gives more probiotic inoculation. In fact a mother's milk consists of up to 40 per cent probiotic content.

2. Probiotics are everywhere.

The largest number of probiotics live in the colon, stomach

(Continued)

and intestines but billions more can reside in the mouth, nose, oesophagus, gums, lungs, vagina, rectum and urinary tract. They can even be found dwelling in joints, armpits, between the toes and under nails.

3. The probiotics in our bodies outweigh our brains.

If the average healthy human body contains around 3kg of probiotic bacteria, and the brain weighs around 1.4kg, the heart around 300g and the liver about 1.5kg, that makes probiotic bacteria one of the largest 'organs' in our body.

4. The probiotics market is colossal.

Probiotics may be everywhere but that doesn't stop us wanting more. The global probiotics food industry is now worth a massive £15 billion and is expected to almost double in size over the next ten years. What's more, over five hundred probiotic food and beverage products have been introduced to the global food market in the last decade. And these numbers, too, are expected to grow.

5. And finally . . . the appendix isn't useless after all.

Long denigrated as being good for nothing, the appendix now appears to have a reason to exist: as a 'safe house' for beneficial bacteria. In 2007 a group of scientists and researchers from Duke University, North Carolina, observed that when the body was under attack by pathogens, the appendix released probiotic bacteria that could counter that specific type of invader. Clever, eh?

21

Why are vitamins added to cornflakes?

NOVELIST SOMERSET MAUGHAM WAS such a fan of the iconic full English breakfast, yet so disparaging of every other kind of British meal, he once advised that 'to eat well in England you should have breakfast three times a day'. And surely he was right. While historically British cuisine has never really lived up to the sky-high benchmark set by its showy continental counterparts, few nations do a breakfast more delicious than a good, honest fry-up – a culinary curiosity held in such high esteem it is emulated, with varying degrees of success, the world over (and yes, that includes France).

But the truth is, owing to the double whammy of increasingly hectic lifestyles and a fixation on the importance of healthy eating, Britons have consigned their most iconic coronary-causing dish to the doldrums. In 1968 approximately half the population tucked into a cooked breakfast on a regular basis; by 1990 this had dropped to a measly 10 per cent. Its replacement? Cereal. For years we've been sold the story that a bowl of cereal with cold milk is one of the healthiest, most wholesome things a parent can feed their child. Indeed so convinced are we by cereal's ability to set us up for the day that the UK is now the largest consumer of cereal in Europe, and it now accounts for over 90 per cent of all breakfasts eaten. Somerset Maugham must be turning in his grave. But if it is so naturally nutritious then why is the UK's favourite cereal, cornflakes, fortified with nutrients such as iron and vitamins? Surely corn contains enough natural goodness without having to be fortified?

It is generally believed this marvel of modern cereal was invented, or rather stumbled upon, in the late nineteenth century by John Harvey Kellogg, a young man from a Seventh-Day Adventist family in the small town of Battle Creek, Michigan. Though as a child he had almost no education, Kellogg miraculously completed a medical degree and became a fanatical advocate of what he called 'biologic living', which involved abstaining from meat, alcohol, tobacco, tea, coffee, eggs and dairy products. The premise of such a diet? That these flavourful foods evoked ungodly passionate thoughts.

In his mid-twenties Kellogg became president of an Adventist sanatorium where he proceeded to impose his austere culinary beliefs on its patients. The problem was, Kellogg's food was so bland nobody would touch it. So he began to think of a new food that was both bland enough not to evoke those passionate thoughts but tasty enough actually to eat. The idea for cornflakes arose on the morning of 8 August 1894 when Kellogg left some cooked wheat to sit while attending to some pressing matters at the sanatorium. When he returned he found that the wheat had gone stale, but being stingy he decided to continue to process it by forcing it through rollers, hoping to obtain some long sheets of dough. To his surprise what he created instead were flakes, which he then proceeded to toast and serve to his patients.

They were a roaring success. Indeed so popular were these crispy flakes of grain that a patent for 'Flaked Cereals and Process of Preparing Same' was filed by Kellogg on 31 May 1895; it was issued on 14 April 1896. It wasn't long before the budding entrepreneur began to experiment with other flaked grains – including, of course, corn. Fast-forward 120 years and Kellogg's Cornflakes are the biggest-selling cereal brand in Europe, estimated to be found in 40 per cent of all UK homes. And off the back of this product Kellogg's has managed to turn itself into one of the largest multinational food producers in the world with over thirty thousand employees, an annual turnover of around $14 billion,

Four Reasons Why Breakfast Really is the Most Important Meal of the Day

Mothers have been extolling the virtues of breakfast to their children since time immemorial. And guess what? According to experts, it turns out they were right all along.

1. Lose weight. A 2003 study in the *American Journal of Epidemiology* showed that people who skip breakfast are 4.5 times more likely to be obese than those who take a morning meal. Why? While asleep your body slows down its metabolic rate. Eating breakfast wakes up your metabolism, helping you to burn calories throughout the day. Moreover, if you skip breakfast you're likely to be so hungry by lunchtime that you'll want to gorge. The same study also showed that eating out for dinner and breakfast is linked with a higher risk of obesity – so probably best to make breakfast at home.

2. Be healthier. A study presented in 2003 at the American Heart Association's annual conference showed that not only are breakfast-eaters less likely to be obese, they're also more likely to have healthy blood sugar levels, reducing the risk of Type 2 diabetes and cardiovascular disease. Moreover, a study in the *American Journal of Clinical Nutrition* showed that breakfast-skippers tend to consume more fat and fewer nutrients like calcium, potassium and fibre than breakfast-eaters, resulting in insulin sensitivity and higher levels of cholesterol.

3. Do better at work and school. Numerous studies have shown that eating a nutritious breakfast can aid concentration and help you to feel more alert. Conversely, those who skip breakfast are more likely to feel apathetic, disinterested and irritable. But it all depends on the type of food you eat. According to a 1999 study in the *International Journal of Food Sciences and Nutrition*, a high-fibre, low-carb breakfast is the way forward.

(Continued)

4. It's an excuse to eat really nice food: What's not to like about oatmeal and eggs? Oatmeal has been shown in many studies to be good at lowering cholesterol levels, and research has also shown that it could help improve children's memory and attention skills when eaten for breakfast. And eating eggs for breakfast has been linked to increased satiety and the consumption of less food throughout the day.

manufacturing plants in some thirty-five countries and a Royal Warrant from none other than Queen Elizabeth II herself. Pretty impressive for a food originally designed to toe the line between bland and edible.

But how are cornflakes actually made? Funnily enough, a large proportion of the 100 million packets of Kellogg's Cornflakes churned out every year start their lives in a factory on the outskirts of Manchester, where the corn arrives in the form of whole yellow tooth-like kernels – just like the ones you find on the cob. Believe it or not, before they make it into your breakfast bowl these kernels are naturally pretty nutritious. The tough outer covering of the kernel is the pericarp, or bran coat, which is primarily made of cellulose. Like starch, cellulose consists of individual sugar molecules chemically linked together. But the way in which sugar molecules in starch and cellulose bind together differs. Your digestive system produces enzymes that quickly and easily break down the chemical bonds in starch, releasing sugar molecules that pass into your bloodstream; these enzymes, however, can't break down the same bonds in cellulose. The bran coat therefore passes through your intestines intact – the reason why you often see sweetcorn in the toilet bowl.

That and what follows may not sound particularly appetizing, but these indigestible husks have their advantages. Although corn's bran coat passes through your gastrointestinal tract without breaking down, the cellulose absorbs water, which keeps your stools soft and promotes regular bowel movements – making it exceptionally good at tackling a whole host of digestive ailments including constipation and haemorrhoids. Additionally, the bulkiness of water-soaked cellulose causes you to feel full for an extended period of time, which may help with weight control. If that isn't enough, corn kernels have another highly nutritious part to them known as the wheatgerm. As the would-be plant portion of the kernel, the wheatgerm is a nutritional powerhouse, packed full of vitamins and other nutrients including folic acid, B vitamins, beta-carotene, protein, vitamin C and essential fats like omega-3.

The bad news is, once the kernels arrive in the factory they swiftly have almost all of this goodness removed. First the husks are discarded to give the cornflakes a smoother texture, then the wheatgerms are squeezed out to give the cornflakes a longer shelf life. What you're left with is the kernel's endosperm, or 'corn grits' as they call it in the industry – the pulpy bit of the kernel that provides starchy nourishment to the wheatgerm. Sadly, this part of the kernel provides no such nourishment to humans as it's around 90 per cent starchy carbohydrates. Not only are corn grits lacking in nourishment they are also largely flavourless, which is why they are then combined with sugar, glucose syrup and salt before being baked for two hours in pressure cookers, rolled into flakes and toasted. With much of the cereal's natural goodness having been removed, it is at this point that cornflakes are sprayed with a combination of nutrients including folic acid and vitamins A, B, C and D.

The other big addition to cornflakes is food-grade iron, and with good reason: a lack of iron remains one of the few nutritional deficiencies in the developed world. Every year hundreds of millions of people, especially children, are affected. And as the compound in red blood cells that carries oxygen from your lungs around your body, it's pretty important stuff. In fact a diet deficient in iron can result in reduced resistance to diseases and increased heart and respiratory rates. Therefore cereal brands that can market their products as high in iron don't just get brownie points from public health officials, they increase sales. But what exactly is food-grade iron? Is it the same kind of iron you find in spinach or a hunk of prime steak? Well, no, it's actually iron filings, made up of tiny particles of pure iron metal (also called elemental iron or reduced iron), processed in a way that renders them tasteless. It may not taste like iron but it certainly acts like it: hover a magnet over your cereal and you should be able to move a few individual flakes.

The fortification of food with vitamins and, er, metal might sound a little sci-fi but it certainly isn't a new concept. One of the first documented examples of food fortification was way back in the early 1900s, when the US government ordered vitamin B3 (niacin) to be added to corn grits – then a staple food for the poor in New Orleans – to help combat the rise of pellagra, a disease caused by chronic lack of vitamin B3. The initiative worked, and after the First World War the British government called for vitamins A and D to be added to margarine because of the unavailability of butter. Then in the 1930s white flour began to be fortified with calcium, iron, thiamine (vitamin B1) and niacin – all things you'll still find in flour today. Indeed these days you'll also find fluoride in tap water, iodine in salt, omega-3 in eggs and cholesterol-lowering stanols in all manner of foods including chocolate, margarine, yoghurts and even orange juice.

As for whether or not the fortification of food is a good thing, well, that's a matter of opinion. It is estimated that more than two billion people worldwide, the vast majority of whom live in developing countries, do not meet their daily dietary requirements for essential vitamins and minerals. The result? Debilitating diseases such as goitre (enlarged thyroid gland), rickets, beriberi (caused by a deficiency in vitamin B1) and pellagra (deficiency in vitamin B3), all of which were common health problems in developed countries until the introduction of fortified foods. Yet the question remains: should we all be exposed to mass medication through artificial means or should we all just be eating the right kinds of food in the first place?

In the Know: Mass Medication

Scientists say fortifying foods with minerals and vitamins saves lives. Critics say it's forced medication. Whatever your view, chances are you eat fortified foods on a daily basis. Here are just a few of them:

Iodine in salt: Iodine deficiency is the most common cause of preventable mental impairment, affecting a third of the world's population. It also causes thyroid problems. Since 1993 the World Health Organization has been conducting a global programme of salt iodization to boost dietary levels. In the UK salt iodization isn't compulsory but added iodine can be found in many brands.

Fluoride: Water fluoridation – the addition of fluoride to a public water supply to reduce tooth decay – is practised by water companies across the UK. In fact around six million people in the UK drink artificially fluoridated tap water.

Stanols and sterols: These cholesterol-lowering substances occur naturally in plant foods such as fruits, vegetables, nuts and seeds. But thanks to fortification you can now find them in a whole host of non-plant foods including yoghurts, margarine, cheese and orange juice.

Riboflavin: This 'forgotten B vitamin' plays an essential role in the body's metabolism, helping to convert the foods you eat into energy for your cells. A deficiency is rare except in those with very poor diets, but riboflavin is still added to many breads and cereals, including Shreddies, Weetabix and Rice Krispies.

Vitamin D: Good for bone health and may help prevent diabetes, heart disease, cancer and multiple sclerosis. Most people should be able to get all the vitamin D they need from the sun, but some, particularly the elderly, the very young and the pregnant, are at risk of deficiency – one of the reasons it is added to many cereals.

(Continued)

Niacin: Added to the staple food corn grits in the early 1900s in the American South to combat pellagra. In Britain it is often added to flour.

Folic acid: Believed to help prevent some birth defects when given to pregnant women. Some think folic acid should be added to flour, as it is in the US.

Iron: It is estimated that around one in ten women and about 25 per cent of pregnant women are deficient in this essential mineral. Flour has been fortified with iron in Britain since the 1930s.

22

How fresh is 'pure squeezed' orange juice?

ORANGE JUICE EXUDES HEALTH and vitality. It's officially one of your 'five a day'. It's sold in juice bars, those wholesome temples of porridge, herbal tea and wheatgrass. Not only that, half-consumed cartons of the stuff are found in almost every fridge in Britain – an eternally present source of liquid vitamin C for the good of the whole family. Indeed we have fallen for orange juice so much, the more hip among us now affectionately refer to it simply as OJ. How many other foods are bestowed with such a touchy-feely abbreviation?

Orange juice is one of the most consumed drinks in the Western world. In the UK alone we gulp down 685 million litres of the stuff every year – that's almost a billion pounds' worth. In 2013 the research company Mintel found that over 80 per cent of people drink fruit juice or smoothies at least once a week and that the orange juice market will grow by 13 per cent by 2018. The reason for such exponential growth? According to the same study, 76 per cent of us are adamant that fruit juice is healthy. But how healthy is it? And is it as fresh as we think it is?

Much of the orange juice we consume in Britain starts life in factories like the Zuvamesa orange juice plant in Valencia, Spain, a factory so large and technologically advanced it has the capacity to produce around 100 million litres of juice every single year. All orange juice production on this scale starts the same way: with the arrival of just-picked oranges, delivered to the factory by truck. So laden are these industrial vehicles with oranges (some can contain as much as 25,000kg of the fruit) they are driven on to hydraulic ramps which tilt the entire truck head over tail, depositing the oranges out of the back end. The oranges are then swiftly put on to huge conveyor belts where a team of workers sort them by hand. Damaged specimens are removed and sent off to be used in the production of animal feed but those deemed good enough to make the grade are washed and sent straight to the juicing section.

The more hi-tech factories, like the Zuvamesa plant, can squeeze over fourteen thousand oranges dry every minute (that's two million kilos in a single twenty-hour shift) with the help of industrial-sized extractors. Once the juice is extracted the pulp is filtered out, placed into containers and stored in a sub-zero cold room (more on that later). The remaining juice is placed into centrifuges and spun at high velocity to remove its essential oils, the majority of which consists of a substance called limone, a colourless liquid that gives oranges their trademark citric aroma. Some of this is kept for later in the process but a large amount is sold off to chemical companies to be incorporated in perfumes, soaps, solvents, household cleaners, stain removers and cosmetics. That's right: no orange juice, no orange-flavoured lip balm.

Next, the juice, now stripped of its pulp and essential oils, is piped off to another part of the factory to be flash-pasteurized at temperatures of around 80– 95°C. This thirty-second blast of heat does two jobs: it kills off any bacteria, delaying the onset of decomposition, and permanently deactivates the fruit's enzymes, which if left intact would cause the juice to separate. But exposure to heat isn't the only process orange juice manufacturers ensure their juice undergoes. Once pasteurized the juice is fed into stainless-steel tanks inside giant cold storage units, some of which contain the equivalent of 40 million one-litre cartons of juice. There, nitrogen is bubbled through the juice to displace any oxygen to further slow down decomposition. While manufacturers aim to shift all their orange juice as quickly as possible it can be stored like this for up to two years without perishing.

The trouble with industrial processing like this is it reduces what is naturally a very lively, zingy product into something rather dull. This is particularly true of pasteurization, which destroys some of the more delicate aromatic components. In fact if you were to taste the juice directly from its storage tank its flavour would resemble an extremely sugary orange-coloured water with only the faintest hint of orange juice. So now for the clever bit. Just before the juice is ready to leave the factory some of the pulp and essential oils removed at the beginning of the squeezing process are reintroduced, thus reuniting the juice with its long-lost texture, flavour and aroma. Amazingly, not all the pulp and oils put into a carton of orange juice come from the same factory, or even the same country. The juice from some factories is made with pulp from Florida, juice from Spain and essential oils from as far away as Brazil. It's all a matter of taste and economy.

So mass-produced orange juice involves a fair amount of technical wizardry before it makes it to the kitchen table. But it's still healthy to drink, right? It is, after all, 100 per cent orange juice. Well, no, not exactly. Though orange juice is rich in vitamin C it is also packed full of sugar, which we all know is linked to diabetes, high blood pressure, heart disease and obesity. A large glass of orange juice typically contains around five teaspoons of the stuff, which pretty much puts it on a par with fizzy soft drinks like Coke and lemonade.

So concerned are experts by the high sugar content of fruit juice that in January 2014 government health tsar Susan Jebb, head of the diet and obesity research group at Oxford University, suggested that the government's official advice that a glass of fruit juice counts towards your recommended minimum five-a-day servings of fruit and vegetables should be scrapped – owing to its high sugar content. What's more, according to obesity expert Robert Lustig, author of *Fat Chance: The Bitter Truth about Sugar*, fruit juice contains so much sugar it is basically a type of poison. This may sound a little over the top, but when you read some of the case studies from Lustig's childhood obesity clinic in San Francisco, it's hard to disagree. One eight-year-old already has high blood pressure thanks to a three-glasses-a-day juice habit. A six-year-old Latino boy came to the clinic weighing 100lb, 'wider than he is tall'. His mother, it turned out, had been letting him drink a gallon of juice a day because a government welfare programme gave it to them for free.

Obviously most of us drink nothing like a gallon of juice a day but according to experts our portions are still too high. It's hard to imagine these days but juice never used to be seen as something you quenched your thirst with; it was more like a vitamin shot, a tiny dose of goodness to be taken when feeling ill. In his influential book *The Care and Feeding of Children* (1894) pioneering paediatrician Luther Emmett Holt recommended giving toddlers no more than the juice of one fourth of one orange per day. Skip to today and you'll find cartons of juice in children's lunchboxes containing the juice of six whole oranges.

But surely the kind of sugar you find in orange juice is healthier than the type of sugar you would typically find in a soft drink? Fruit juice typically contains two different kinds of sugar: glucose and fructose. When you consume glucose, a type of sugar found in lots of sugary foods, your body releases insulin, which causes the cells in the liver, muscle and fat tissue to take up the glucose from the blood and convert it to glycogen that can then be stored in the liver and muscles for the body's use when it needs energy. When there is excess glucose the body converts it to fat, which is deposited subcutaneously (i.e. it sits just under your skin). This might sound unhealthy but the general consensus among experts is that fructose or 'fruit sugar' is even worse. The problem with fructose is that humans aren't exactly geared up to consume it because unlike glucose it doesn't cause insulin to be released. Instead all fructose is metabolized by the liver, so an excess of it contributes to an increase in visceral fat (the kind of fat you find around the vital organs). As a result, heavy fructose consumption can lead to cirrhosis of the liver, obesity, cardiovascular damage and even liver cancer. Moreover the damage caused by fructose is very hard to spot, mainly because those suffering from it tend not to *look* fat. Due to increasing fruit juice and smoothie sales as well as the inclusion of fructose as a sweetener in many processed foods, it is estimated that we now consume around three times more fructose than we did fifteen years ago – a fact many believe is a public health time bomb.

So how much is too much? The British Dietetic Association says that because of its high fructose levels we should drink only one 150ml glass of fruit juice a day. The best way to cut down our daily intake is to dilute juice with water, or stop eating other high-fructose foods like corn syrup, agave nectar, honey, molasses and maple syrup. And whatever you do, never use fruit juice as a replacement for actual fruit. In 2012 researchers from the UK, USA and Singapore found that people who ate whole fruit, especially blueberries, grapes and apples, were less likely to get Type 2 diabetes, which is obesity-related. Those who drank fruit juice were at increased risk. This is because when you eat a whole piece of fruit the fructose in it comes equipped with fibre, giving your liver time to fully metabolize it. Smoothies are not much better, no matter how attractive the packaging, because when fruit is blended the insoluble fibre is torn to smithereens. So while an apple a day may help to keep the doctor away be sure not to overdo it on the juicy stuff.

Four foods with Big Surprises

The diet industry is booming, yet we've never been fatter. Could 'healthy choice' foods have something to do with it?

Granola: The vast majority of us consider this combination of cereal, honey, dried fruit and nuts a healthy and delicious breakfast option. And why not? Most granolas feature energy-giving fibre-rich oats as their primary ingredient. But having oats centre-stage doesn't automatically make granola a health food, and definitely doesn't make it low-calorie. In reality most granolas are classified as high-sugar, with more than 12.5g of sugar per 100g, much of which has been deliberately added to make it taste more palatable than the stuff found in health food shops. And don't be fooled by the addition of honey – it's still a sugar.

Low-fat food: Reduced-fat foods may sound like a great idea (especially if you're dieting) but while less fat in your diet can be a good thing, products with these labels usually come at a price. For example, when the fat is removed from a product, its sodium and sugar content are often bumped up. What's more, not all fats are bad. While the consumption of too many saturated fats (such as butter) and trans fats (including partially hydrogenated vegetable oils) has been linked to chronic conditions like diabetes and heart disease, unsaturated fats such as omega-3 fatty acids are essential to a healthy diet.

Energy bars: Many energy and protein-rich 'sports' bars are marketed as 'fuel for athletes' but the truth is Brits of all activity levels consume them, wrongly believing they are a form of healthy snack. In reality energy bars are simply a portable way of delivering the highest number of calories possible in the shortest amount of time, which is helpful if you're an endurance athlete but not a great idea if you're sat in front of a

(Continued)

computer all day. Many sports bars are fortified with nutrients, too, which if you already have a healthy diet can send your vitamin levels rocketing above your recommended daily allowance.

Frozen yoghurt: You may feel virtuous ordering a creamy white swirl of frozen yoghurt from any one of the 'real' yoghurt vendors popping up across Britain; much of it is packed full of probiotics and is a lot lighter than your average dollop of ice cream, right? Not so fast. Frozen yoghurt may be relatively low in saturated fat but in terms of calories it isn't far behind ice cream, especially once you start adding toppings. What's more, some frozen yoghurts have been found to contain a whole host of additives and artificial flavourings. As for probiotics: natural yoghurt may be brimming with gut-friendly bacteria but according to some experts once you expose them to extreme temperatures – by freezing them, for instance – they become all but useless.

23

Is it true that a glass of red wine a day is good for you?

THESE DAYS FEW OF us challenge the idea that a glass or two of plonk each day will help to keep the doctor at bay. But what most don't know is that our current image of red wine as a healer can be traced back to a specific date in very recent history: 30 August 1991, the day French scientist Dr Serge Renaud coined the term 'French Paradox'.

Renaud used the phrase on US TV show *60 Minutes* to summarize the curious phenomenon that French people have some of the lowest levels of heart disease in Europe despite having a diet rich in saturated fats – thus contradicting the widely accepted belief that the consumption of such fats causes heart disease. It is a paradox that continues to perplex experts. In 2002 the average French person consumed 108g per day of fat from animal sources, while the average American consumed only 72g. The French eat four times as much butter, 60 per cent more cheese and nearly three times as much pork. Yet, according to data from the British Heart Foundation, rates of death from coronary heart disease among American males aged 35–74 were 115 per 100,000 people, but only 83 per 100,000 in France. The reason, according to Renaud, is regular, moderate consumption of red wine with meals. It may not sound like a revolutionary concept today but prior to the airing of *60 Minutes* almost all medical research treated alcohol as a risk factor, never something to be enjoyed regularly as part of a healthy lifestyle.

Renaud's argument not only dramatically increased red wine sales in Britain and America, it launched a new wave of research exploring the benefits of wine and alcohol that continues today.

Renaud undoubtedly changed red wine's image as we moved into the twenty-first century but it would be wrong to give him all the credit. Wine has a long and proud history as a form of medication. Tablets from Sumerian culture and papyri from Ancient Egypt dating from 2200 BC include recipes for wine-based medicines, making wine one of the oldest documented man-made remedies. Even with the rise of the Ancient Greeks and their more enlightened approach to medicine, wine retained its importance. The Greek physician Hippocrates recommended wine as part of a healthy diet and advocated its use as a disinfectant for wounds, as well as a liquid to mix other drugs into for easier consumption. He also prescribed wine as a cure for a number of ailments ranging from diarrhoea and lethargy to pain during childbirth. The Ancient Romans embraced wine as a form of medicine too. In his first-century work *De Medicina* the great medical writer Aulus Cornelius Celsus detailed a long list of Greek and Roman wines used for medicinal purposes. And while treating gladiators in Anatolia, the Greek physician Galenus would use wine as a disinfectant for all types of wounds, even going so far as to soak exposed guts in it before returning them to the body. It is claimed that during his four years in the amphitheatre only five deaths occurred, compared to sixty deaths under the watch of the non-wine-touting physician before him.

It continued to be pretty much plain sailing for vino until the early 1900s and the rise of the Temperance movement, which made its name by decrying alcohol. As a result public opinion turned against the consumption of alcohol of any kind and interest in wine as a healthy drink waned. A further knock to wine's healthy image came in the mid-twentieth century when experts began to study the effects on health of alcohol – and it wasn't good news. Numerous studies emerged highlighting the fact that excessive consumption of alcohol can lead to all manner of horrendous problems including strokes, heart disease, dementia, high blood pressure, osteoporosis, liver disease and reduced fertility; more recently, studies have linked alcohol consumption with an increased risk of breast, colon, oesophageal and stomach cancer. Indeed alcohol is considered so toxic to the human body it is classified as a Group 1 carcinogen by the World Health Organization, putting it alongside plutonium-239, hepatitis C, asbestos and mustard gas. Not sounding too good for the pro-red wine camp so far.

It is for these reasons the UK recommends that men consume only three to four units of alcohol per day (roughly a single large 250ml glass of red wine); for women the figure is no more than two to three units – roughly one 175ml glass of wine. Such recommendations aren't a new thing either. The Greek poet Eubulus believed that three kylix drinking cups' worth of wine was the ideal amount to consume (which is why today the standard 750ml wine bottle contains roughly the volume of three Ancient Greek kylix cups). In his *c.* 375 BC play *Semele or Dionysus*, Eubulus has the character Dionysus say, 'Three bowls do I mix for the temperate: one to health, which they empty first, the second to love and pleasure, the third to sleep. When this bowl is drunk up, wise guests go home. The fourth bowl is ours no longer, but belongs to violence; the fifth to uproar, the sixth to drunken revel, the seventh to black eyes, the eighth is the policeman's, the ninth belongs to biliousness, and the tenth to madness and hurling the furniture.' Some things never change, eh?

The general consensus among experts (and Greek playwrights) is that while excessive alcohol is bad for you (throat cancer, heart disease, black eyes, furniture throwing and suchlike) it's less harmful in moderation. Certainly new research suggests that moderate wine drinking (a glass or two a day) may indeed be actively good for us, as Dr Renaud asserted. In his seminal book *The Wine Diet*, British professor Roger Corder explained that the flavour of red wine is heavily dependent on the variety of polyphenols, or flavonoids – natural chemicals from the grape pips and skins – they contain. A specific group of polyphenols called procyanidins is believed to be important for improving blood-vessel function and preventing heart disease, diabetes, macular degeneration, dementia and more. The most procyanidin-rich wines tend to be those in which the grapes, including skins and seeds, have remained in contact with the wine during fermentation and afterwards. One of the wine-growing regions to boast the highest concentrations of procyanidins in its grapes is Madiran in the Pyrenees: wines from this area contain up to ten times more beneficial compounds than their counterparts from other parts of the world. 'It's no wonder that the Madiran area has double the French national average of men aged ninety, and this is despite regularly eating foods high in saturated fat, such as cassoulet,' says Professor Corder.

Another of red wine's health benefits is believed to stem from the compound resveratrol, also found in the skins and seeds of grapes. Since red wines, particularly tannic varieties, typically enjoy extended contact time with the grapes' skins during fermentation they will naturally have higher levels of resveratrol than white wines. Resveratrol is a naturally occurring, powerful antioxidant produced by grape vines to counter the damaging effects of free radicals caused by UV light, pathogens, pollution and environmental toxins. These same free radicals can cause damage to humans as well and are frequently blamed for everything from the ageing process to heart disease, diabetes and Alzheimer's. Thankfully, studies have shown that a diet rich in antioxidants can help render free radicals neutral.

In a 2006 study on the benefits of resveratrol conducted by Harvard Medical School, mice fed on high-calorie diets along with high concentrations of resveratrol gained less weight, had fewer insulin-dependent issues and suffered from fewer cardiovascular-related problems, all while enjoying a longer lifespan. What's more, research carried out at Cornell University indicates that resveratrol has the unique ability to decrease plaque formation in animal brains as they age, highlighting the potential for the same in Alzheimer's patients. Researchers at the University of Leicester are looking at whether resveratrol could one day be developed into a cancer-preventing drug. Experimenting on mice in the lab, they've found that a daily amount of resveratrol equivalent to two glasses of wine can halve the rate of bowel tumours.

But hold on there. Don't see this as a green light to start gorging on red wine. Professor Karen Brown from the department of cancer studies and molecular medicine at Leicester says her research must not be misconstrued. 'We're not saying red wine can prevent cancer – we are looking at the pure compound. Alcohol is not good for cancer, but it just so happens that red wine contains resveratrol.' Dr Emma Smith, science communications officer at Cancer Research UK, backs this up, saying it is a mistake to drink red wine and believe it is doing good. 'Red wine contains only very small amounts of resveratrol and people shouldn't drink wine in an attempt to get any health benefits. It's important to remember that, even in moderate amounts, alcohol increases the risk of several cancers and has been estimated to cause around 12,500 cases of cancer a year in the UK.'

A little perplexed by the conflicting advice? What we can be certain of is that if you are intent on regularly drinking red wine then you are far more likely to reap any potential benefits by enjoying it in moderation. One recent study shows that moderate drinking (one alcoholic beverage per day in midlife) boosts the likelihood of 'successful ageing' with less chance of cancer, heart disease or significant cognitive decline. But drink any more than this and you risk undoing some of the wine's health-giving properties. The bottom line: if red wine isn't your thing, there's no need to make yourself sip it just for its health benefits. But if you love a drop of Pinot Noir, there's something to be said for having a guilt-free glass with dinner most nights.

A Brief History of Wine as Medicine

2200 BC: Tablets from Sumerian culture and papyri from Ancient Egypt include recipes for wine-based medicines.

400 BC: Hippocrates, the 'Father of Medicine', recommends wine as part of a healthy diet and advocates its use as a cure for various ailments and a disinfectant for wounds, as well as a medium in which to mix other drugs.

AD 1: In *De Medicina*, Celsus details Greek and Roman wines used for medicinal purposes.

AD 2: In his first epistle to Timothy, Paul the Apostle recommends that his young colleague drink a little wine every now and then for the benefit of his stomach and digestion.

AD 150: While treating gladiators, Galenus uses wine as a disinfectant for all types of wounds. During his four years tending to gladiators only five deaths occur.

860–1037: After the fall of the Roman Empire, Europe enters the 'Dark Ages' and much medical knowledge is lost. However, a number of eminent Arabic doctors including Rhazes (860–932), Albucasis (936–1013) and Avicenna (980–1037) continue to use wine to treat infection.

1500: Hieronymus Brunschwig, a surgeon in the Alsatian army, promotes a mixture of strong Gascony wine, brandy and herbs, which he calls 'Aqua Vitae Composite', for cleansing wounds. The concoction is also said to 'cure palsy, putteth away ringworms, expel poison and it was most wholesome for the stomach, heart and liver'.

1510: In medieval Europe monks combine plants and herbs with wine to create different medicines. Each different order has its own special recipe, some of which have evolved into present-day liqueurs such as D.O.M. Bénédictine, which was first made in a Benedictine abbey in France in 1510.

(Continued)

1892: Wine is used to sterilize water during the Hamburg cholera epidemic in order to control the spread of the disease.

Early 1900s: The Temperance movement gains popularity partly by touting the ills of alcoholism – which officially becomes defined as a disease. Studies of the effects of alcohol on health cause many in the medical community to reconsider the role of wine in medicine.

Mid-1900s: Health advocates link alcohol consumption with a huge variety of ailments including strokes, skin infections, liver damage, infertility, cancer, high blood pressure and even brain damage.

1991: US news programme *60 Minutes* airs a piece about the 'French Paradox'. Scientist Serge Renaud proposes that moderate consumption of red wine is a risk-reducing factor for the French and that it could have more health benefits yet to be studied. Sales of red wine in the US jump by 44 per cent.

2000–present: There is renewed interest in the health benefits of wine, mainly as a result of increasing research suggesting moderate wine drinkers enjoy lower mortality rates than teetotallers.

24

Are there any strawberries in strawberry flavouring?

B E THEY BLITZED INTO milkshakes, blended into yoghurts, boiled into jam or simply served up straight with a generous dollop of double cream, there is nothing more evocative of a British summer than strawberries. The trouble is, they have a painfully short season. Officially the berries are grown from April through to October, but many of us feel in our hearts they're only at their best for the fleeting twelve-week period between June and August. There are foreign imports, of course, many of which are available all year round – but let's be honest, none lives up to the sweet juiciness of their in-season counterparts. So how come we can buy consistently delicious strawberry-flavoured foods all year round, many of which proudly boast the words 'naturally flavoured'?

It's easy to think of food flavourings as a new thing, the work of hi-tech multinational companies attempting to pep up the innate blandness of their processed produce. But humans have been sprucing up their food like this for thousands of years. Indeed the roots of the flavour industry date as far back as the Ancient Egyptians, who were the first to embrace fragrant spices, herbs and aromatic oils to create elaborate perfumes and flavours. A little later herbal distillation was invented by the Ancient Greeks, allowing alchemists to separate flavours into specific compounds. Indeed this same process is still in use today. Many of the essential oils and aromas currently used in flavourings were originally discovered through distillation in pharmacies in the sixteenth and seventeenth centuries. The biggest revolution in the world of flavouring, however, came during the 1960s, a decade that saw the rise of supermarkets and processed foods, which meant that for the first time people were eating non-local produce. The trouble with food that doesn't go directly from field to fork? Loss of flavour. On the back of this simple fact a whole industry was born.

To understand how food companies manipulate flavours it helps to know how humans experience them in the first place. First, we don't really taste things at all – we smell them. Indeed the aroma of food can be responsible for as much as 90 per cent of its overall flavour. The theory goes that humans developed a sense of taste to avoid being poisoned: edible things in the natural world generally taste sweet, while toxins often taste bitter. But our taste buds are pretty rudimentary things that act more like a safety net than anything else. They can only really tell the difference between sweet, salty, sour, bitter and savoury (or 'umami' as it's officially called). In comparison to this our olfactory system (basically our sense of smell) can perceive thousands upon thousands of different chemical aromas. Therefore 'flavour' is primarily the smell of gases being released by the chemicals you've just put in your mouth, explains Eric Schlosser in his book *Fast Food Nation*. 'The act of drinking, sucking, or chewing a substance releases its volatile gases,' he says. 'They flow out of the mouth and up the nostrils, or up the passageway in the back of the mouth, to a thin layer of nerve cells called the olfactory epithelium, located at the base of the nose, right between the eyes. The brain combines the complex smell signals from the epithelium with the simple taste signals from the tongue, assigns a flavour to what's in your mouth, and decides if it's something you want to eat.' Try remembering that the next time you tuck into a packet of pork scratchings.

These volatile gases, also known as aroma compounds, can be found in almost every kind of food and drink. Quantities vary wildly, however. Foods made with the help of heat, like bread, beer, cocoa and tea, typically have extremely high levels of aroma compounds, around eight hundred of them in some cases, which goes a long way to explaining why we find the smell of bakeries, pubs and cafés so enticing. A relatively high number of compounds are also present in fruits and vegetables. In an apple, for example, you will typically find around thirty different aroma compounds. In something like a strawberry you can find as many as 350 – which is part of the reason they taste so good.

So how on earth do you extract several hundred volatile aroma compounds from a strawberry and insert them into a processed food like a milkshake or a boiled sweet? The simplest, most obvious way to do it is by using actual strawberries. Indeed this is so easy you can do it at home. Simply chop up a punnet of strawberries, heat them until they soften, then squeeze out their red juice with the help of a cheesecloth (for a more in-depth method, see the following page). And there you go, you have yourself some strawberry extract, which can then be added to anything in need of a strawberry-flavoured hit.

While it is possible to find products on the market flavoured with 100 per cent fruit, the vast majority of flavours you find in processed food are manufactured in laboratories by scientists known as flavourists. With the help of a bit of biochemistry these boffins extract aroma compounds from thousands of natural sources such as plants, vegetables and different foods then combine some of them to recreate specific flavours. The remarkable thing is, this method doesn't require the use of compounds derived from the food they are trying to mimic. Raspberry flavouring, for example, may include an ingredient called castoreum derived from the scent gland of a beaver yet contain absolutely nothing derived from a raspberry. As for strawberry flavouring, this too can be created using hundreds of different and unusual aroma compounds, none of which come from strawberries. Here are the five key chemical compounds usually found in strawberry flavouring: furanyl (a by-product of cooked sugar, said to have an aroma reminiscent of burnt meat); cis-3-hexenal (a colourless liquid

DIY: Natural Strawberry Extract

Add a whole new dimension to whipped cream, vanilla icing, muffins, cookies, milkshakes and meringues with the help of this 100 per cent natural strawberry extract.

Things you'll need:

500g strawberries	*colander*
1 cup of water	*cheesecloth/muslin*
½ cup of sugar	*knife*
chopping board	*airtight container*

1. Wash the strawberries, cut away their green tops, then slice into small chunks.

2. Place the strawberry pieces into a saucepan with the water and sugar. Cover the pan, put on a medium heat and bring to a simmer.

3. Cook the strawberries for about thirty minutes or until they start to become very moist and fall apart to the touch.

4. Line the colander with the cheesecloth/muslin and place it over the container to catch the liquid. Pour the cooked strawberries into the colander to separate the liquid from the solids. Squeeze any excess juices from the cheesecloth into the container.

5. Pour the liquid back into the saucepan and leave it to simmer uncovered on a medium heat. Cook the liquid until it is reduced to about a quarter of a cup. (Reducing the liquid evaporates any excess water, concentrating the flavour.)

6. Store the extract in an airtight container in the refrigerator for up to two months and use it as you would use commercially made extract.

(Continued)

Tips: Add less sugar if you prefer a less sweet extract. The extract will stain clothes and skin. It will also tint food items pink when used in recipes.

distilled from peppermint oil and famed for its intense odour of freshly cut green grass – also one of the major volatile compounds found in ripe tomatoes, where it acts as a pheromone to attract pollinating insects); ethyl butyrate (a chemical with a sweet, creamy aroma commonly made through the fermentation of dairy products); gamma decalactone (a by-product of fermented castor oil with a strong peachy aroma); and finally 2-methyl butyric acid (a chemical with a sour fruity aroma that occurs naturally in beer and tobacco). None of these chemicals alone smells anything like strawberries, but once combined they mimic the aroma perfectly.

But why go to all this bother just to recreate the flavour of something available to us naturally? The answer is: cost. 'The human nose can detect aromas present in quantities of a few parts per trillion – an amount equivalent to 0.000000000003 per cent,' says Eric Schlosser. 'The chemical that provides the dominant flavour of a bell pepper, for example, can be tasted in amounts as low as .02 parts per billion; one drop is sufficient to add flavour to five average-size swimming pools. As a result, the amount of flavour additives required in processed foods is often so low it costs less than its packaging.' What's more, many argue it would be a huge waste of natural resources to produce all flavourings from raw ingredients; and unlike actual strawberries, flavourings of this kind are available all year round. Definitely a bonus if you're a large-scale food processor.

So if 'natural flavouring' doesn't actually require any ingredients derived from the food it is trying to mimic, where does that leave artificial flavours? According to the US Code of Federal Regulations, a natural flavour is 'the essential oil, oleoresin, essence or extractive, protein hydrolysate, distillate or any product of roasting, heating or enzymolysis, which contains the flavouring constituents derived from a spice, fruit or fruit juice, vegetable or vegetable juice, edible yeast, herb, bark, bud, root, leaf or similar plant material, meat, seafood, poultry, eggs, dairy products, or fermentation products thereof, whose significant function in food is flavouring rather than nutritional'. In the real world this means that artificial flavours are those that are made from chemicals produced in a laboratory and not by nature.

However, while synthetically produced flavours may sound less appetizing they are essentially exactly the same as those produced by nature because a given flavour can only ever be made with a select group of chemicals. Whether these chemicals are made in a lab or by nature makes not a bean of difference. In fact, if anything, man-made flavours are considered better. Some even argue that natural flavours are unethical because they are sometimes sourced from endangered plants or animals. Natural coconut flavourings, for example, depend on a chemical called massoya lactone which comes from the bark of the massoya tree, which grows in Malaysia. Collecting this natural chemical kills the tree because harvesters must remove the bark first. What's more, the production of natural flavourings generally consumes larger amounts of energy. Completely natural strawberry flavouring (for example) has to be derived from plants that have been fed, grown, harvested, transported and processed. The creation of a synthetic version requires far less energy.

Finally, though health fanatics are often wary of anything produced in a lab, synthetically produced flavourings are considered by some to be safer than their natural counterparts. When making a flavour, the flavourist always begins by researching which chemicals could be used to make the desired flavour. He or she then simplifies the components found in, say, real strawberries, to eliminate those chemicals that make little contribution to taste. Nature has no such restrictions on toxins, yet in many countries such as the US artificial flavours require safety testing but natural flavours don't.

The Lowdown on Food Flavouring

What is taste? Our olfactory system is many times more sensitive than our gustatory (tasting) equipment. 'Flavour' is primarily the smell of volatile gases being released by the food you've just put in your mouth.

What is a flavourant? This term is used in the fragrance and flavours industry to refer to edible chemicals and extracts that alter the flavour of food through the sense of smell.

How are flavourants created? Most food companies do not create their own flavours but instead employ the help of specialist scientists known as flavourists. To produce a 'natural' flavour, different aroma compounds are extracted from natural substances using solvent extraction, distillation or force (i.e. squeezing them out). These chemicals are then combined until the desired flavour is achieved. To produce artificial flavours, flavourists follow the same process but use aroma compounds created in a laboratory.

Are natural flavours fundamentally different to artificial flavours? Everything is a chemical when you break it down. For instance, salt is a chemical; it has a specific molecular structure that helps us identify it as salt. The same can be said for flavours: they are chemicals with specific structures. Natural strawberry flavour could be (and sometimes is) chemically identical to artificial strawberry flavour; the only difference is that the natural strawberry flavour came from something edible found in nature and the artificial flavour came from something built synthetically in a lab.

So, 'natural' strawberry flavouring, it turns out, doesn't require a single molecule of a real strawberry. Not only that, 'artificial' strawberry flavouring (considered by some to be safer and more flavoursome) can be created entirely in a lab. Sounds like a win-win situation, right? Critics of food flavouring think not. Their argument is that if we all ate fresh, healthy, ethically produced food there wouldn't be any need for flavourings of any kind. Food is brimming with all the flavour nature intended, they remind us. Now there's some food for thought.

25

Is it safe to reheat rice?

RICE IS A STAPLE food for nearly one half of the world's population, providing more than a fifth of the total calories consumed world-wide. Our appetite for this grain is so voracious it is cultivated across 150 million hectares of land on every continent on Earth except Antarctica; annual global production is a colossal 730 million tons. Brits alone consume a belly-bloating 5kg of rice each a year – which considering that cooked rice swells to at least three times its original weight is rather a lot.

Given that we consume such vast amounts of rice you'd think we'd know everything about it. Yet one of the most common culinary conundrums seems to be the age-old question of 'Do I or don't I risk eating leftover rice?' It's perfectly understandable why most of us haven't a clue what the correct answer is, however. While the rumour goes that eating reheated rice can cause everything from severe food poisoning to full-blown death, we all know at least one or two thrifty cooks who regularly eat leftover rice and are still here to tell the tale. More baffling still is the emergence in recent years of pre-cooked rice in pouches, which we are told is perfectly safe to reheat at home. So what exactly is going on here?

The sad truth is that food poisoning is a huge problem, rearing its ugly head in almost every region on Earth. According to the World Health Organization (WHO), approximately 1.8 million children in developing countries die each year from diarrhoeal disease caused by microbiological agents, mostly originating in food and water. Western countries are not immune to the perils either: one person in three in industrialized countries is likely to be affected by a foodborne illness each year. In the USA, some 76 million cases of food poisoning, resulting in 325,000 hospitalizations and 5,000 deaths, are estimated to occur each year, while in the UK there are an estimated 1.7 million cases annually (that's a whopping 33,160 cases every week). The overall cost to the National Health Service? Around £500 million a year.

The cause of all this is food contamination, which in turn is usually caused by bacteria, though it can be caused by parasites and viruses too. Nobody knows for sure but there are believed to be trillions of species of bacteria on Earth. Most cases of food poisoning, however, can be blamed on just five or six, campylobacter, salmonella, listeria and E. coli among them (see following page).

Poorly stored and undercooked meat (particularly poultry) is responsible for significant amounts of food poisoning in the UK, but around a quarter of a million cases are caused by reheated rice. This is all thanks to a bacterium known as *Bacillus cereus*, found in the soil and dust of almost all rice-growing regions around the world. Individual rice grains may look smooth to the naked eye, but inspect them through a microscope and you'll see hundreds of valley-like fissures, each one lined with thousands of *B. cereus* spores. A normal bacterium in its spore is a bit like a chick in its egg – it has its protective outer layer and doesn't need any nutrients or water from outside in order to survive. But the outer shell of *B. cereus* is more like the wall of a nuclear bunker than an eggshell: no amount of washing will remove it and it can even tolerate boiling water.

In dry conditions the bacteria stay in their spores; only when their surroundings are warm and wet will they emerge to grow, breed and reproduce. Unfortunately for us, every time we cook rice we create the conditions these bacteria need to thrive. Most of the time the bacteria have no effect on us, mainly because the rice is consumed so soon after being heated they haven't had time to reproduce. Leave the rice to sit at

In the Know: Britain's Worst Bacterial Offenders

Typically, food poisoning causes gastroenteritis – an infection of the gut, which then leads to diarrhoea and vomiting. Many of the UK's estimated 1.7 million cases of food poisoning a year are caused by the following culprits. The good news is they can all be avoided by following storage instructions, not using food past its sell-by date, and thorough cooking.

Campylobacter: In the UK campylobacter is the most common bacterial offender, responsible for around 460,000 cases of food poisoning, 22,000 hospitalizations and 110 deaths each year. Campylobacter bacteria are usually found on raw or undercooked meat (particularly poultry) and in unpasteurized milk and untreated water. Undercooked chicken liver and liver pâté are also common sources.

Salmonella: Salmonella bacteria are commonly found in the guts of many animals, including farm animals and pets. As a result salmonella can potentially contaminate dairy products and meat (particularly poultry).

Listeria: Listeria bacteria can be found in a range of chilled ready-to-eat foods including pre-packed sandwiches, pâté, butter, soft cheeses like Brie and Camembert (and others with a similar rind), blue cheese, cooked sliced meats and smoked salmon. That's why all of these foods should be eaten by their use-by dates.

E. coli: *Escherichia coli* bacteria are found in the digestive systems of many animals, including humans. Most strains are harmless but some can cause serious illness. The vast majority of *E. coli* food poisoning occurs after eating under-cooked beef (particularly mince, burgers and meatballs) or drinking unpasteurized milk.

Viruses: The virus most commonly behind gastrointestinal

(Continued)

illness is the norovirus, which is easily transmitted from person to person, via contaminated food or water. Raw shellfish, particularly oysters (see chapter 13), can be a source of viral contamination. The Food Standards Agency (FSA) advises that older people, pregnant women, very young children and people who are unwell should avoid eating raw or lightly cooked shellfish to reduce their risk of getting food poisoning.
Parasites: In the UK food poisoning from parasites is rare. It is much more common in the developing world. Toxoplasmosis is the most likely cause of parasitical food poisoning in the UK, caused by a parasite found in the digestive systems of many animals, particularly cats. Humans can get toxoplasmosis by consuming undercooked contaminated meat, or food or water tainted with the faeces of infected cats.

room temperature overnight, however, and you give the bacteria every chance to multiply. To add insult to injury, as these little nasties swell in numbers they also excrete a harmful toxin known as cereulide. This is why anyone foolhardy enough to consume improperly stored rice could be in for some abdominal pains and a bout of projectile vomiting (as a result of the toxin) as well as watery and explosive diarrhoea (as a result of the bacteria) – so that's both ends covered then. Moreover, once you've made the mistake of leaving rice out at room temperature for too long there's absolutely nothing you can do to make it safe to eat again. Even reheating improperly stored rice to a high temperature (anything over 63°C) won't help because though the heat will kill the bacteria now that they are out of their bunker-like spores, it won't destroy the toxin. Worse still, once you've got food poisoning there's not a whole lot you can do about it apart from rest (between trips to the toilet), drink lots of water and avoid food. Indeed the only redeeming quality of this bacterial double-whammy is that symptoms generally only last around twenty-four hours. If they don't, it's time for a trip to the doctor.

Number Cruncher: Rice

40,000 – estimated number of varieties of rice. Of these, more than a hundred are grown worldwide but only around 10 per cent are marketed and sold.
730 million – tons of rice produced globally in 2012
100 – number of countries that cultivate rice
29,000 – number of grains in one pound of long-grain rice
5 – kilos of rice the average person in the UK eats each year
96 – percentage of the world's rice that is eaten in the area in which it is grown

As far as bacteria go, then, these little guys and their excretions are pretty damn hardy, not only capable of surviving starvation and dehydration but extreme temperatures too. So how come our supermarkets are lined with unrefrigerated pre-cooked rice? If all grains of rice contain millions of bacteria that are awoken once cooked then surely this stuff is a public health crisis waiting to happen?

Luckily, producers of this kind of rice take care of the bacteria long before they reach your home. All pre-cooked rice is processed in sterile hi-tech factories. These places are so 'bio-secure' that any visitors are strictly required to don full-body protective suits and are blasted prior to entry with pure oxygen to remove any loose fibres. The job of these factories is to stop *Bacillus cereus* in its tracks before it has the chance to germinate and produce the toxins that can make us run for the toilet. They do this by exposing the grains of rice to extremely hot steam. Normally, of course, water evaporates into steam at 100°C but this steam is pressurized, meaning they can bump the temperature up to a scorching 140°C. This super-hot steam penetrates all the spores, killing the bacteria within. And no bacteria means no toxins.

Finally, because there's always a minuscule chance that some bacteria have seen off this blast of heat, the rice undergoes a process known as nitrogen flushing: every packet is pumped full of nitrogen to flush out the oxygen, making it near impossible for any bacteria to survive. Nitrogen gas may sound like a nasty preservative to avoid at all costs but it is in fact incredibly safe. Indeed nitrogen gas makes up 78 per cent of all the air we breathe. So, thanks to this process you can tuck into your packet of pre-cooked rice safe in the knowledge that the dreaded *B. cereus* has been sent packing.

One question remains, of course: is it safe to leave this kind of rice out all night at room temperature and then consume it the following day? You'd think so given the facts of its sterilization. Unfortunately there is no simple answer to this. Different manufacturers prepare their pre-cooked rice in slightly different ways, meaning you can never be 100 per cent certain the rice will stay germ-free. The general consensus, therefore, is that if you want to stay on the safe side, always store and cook it properly.

But if reheating rice is unsafe, what about all those people who do it on a regular basis yet seem not to suffer the faintest hint of diarrhoea or projectile vomiting? The good news is that rice *can* be reheated and eaten but *only* if it's been stored and cooked in the correct way. Indeed restaurants often reheat rice without causing food poisoning. The key to safe rice, say chefs, is storage and temperature control. All rice should be kept bone dry, cooked thoroughly to a temperature of at least 75°C and then served immediately. If rice is not to be served straight away it should be kept at 63°C or above or cooled to at least 15°C as quickly as possible. The best way to do this is by placing the rice in a colander or sieve and running it under cold water for a couple of minutes. The rice will then be ready to put straight into the fridge. Reducing the temperature of the rice like this means that the bacteria don't have time to multiply and produce toxins. Nevertheless, it is strongly recommended that properly stored leftover rice is consumed within one or two days.

Finally, if you have some leftover rice from a takeaway (as an exceedingly large number of us often seem to) you should throw it away immediately. Many takeaway restaurants make their rice in bulk and then reheat it as and when they need it. And rice should never be reheated twice.

So there it is. You can reheat rice just as long as you cool it quickly after cooking, refrigerate it, use it up within a day or so, and reheat it until piping hot. Best of all, just cook the correct amount of rice in the first place. Not that that's likely to happen any time soon.

How to Avoid Dodgy Rice in Five Steps

Avoid adding your name to the UK's annual food poisoning list by following these simple steps:

1. Moist conditions cause the bacteria in rice to germinate, which in turn produces harmful toxins, so always keep rice dry by storing it in a sealed container.

2. Always cook rice thoroughly (to at least 75°C) and serve immediately.

3. If rice is not to be served straight away, keep it at or above 63°C or cool it quickly by running under cold water then refrigerate within sixty minutes.

4. Only keep cooked rice refrigerated for a maximum of two days.

5. Rice is always best served fresh, but if it is to be reheated ensure it is piping hot (75°C or above) throughout before being served, and never reheat twice.

26

How much cream is in ice cream?

IT IS SAID THAT humans have a natural inclination towards consuming ice cream; it starts at birth and never really leaves us. One theory has it that we simply cannot get enough of foods that readily change texture in our mouths: as ice cream melts from solid to liquid it fills us with some kind of sensual euphoria that keeps us going back for more. Others posit that mankind's addiction to cold cream is all to do with fat: when you lick a dollop of ice cream its emulsified fats envelop your tongue, making your taste buds tingle in sweet, syrupy delight. Finally, and importantly, ice cream is easy to digest. It places extremely low on something called the satiety index, which in the real world means you can eat a hell of a lot of it without feeling full.

But, while all of the above are probably true, is it not ice cream's delightful simplicity that makes it so appealing? There can't be a child in Britain who doesn't know that ice cream is made by freezing gloriously rich cream. After all, it's there in the name, isn't it? Well, perhaps not. The truth is, many people would fast lose their appetite if they knew what actually went into some of the millions of tubs of ice cream that are sold from supermarket freezer cabinets every year. Indeed most surprising of all are the ingredients that are left out.

Foods that Don't Do What They Say on the Tin

The term 'ice cream' may be misleading, but the names of these foods are just plain wrong.

Welsh rabbit
What you'd expect it to be: A medieval Welsh dish made using rabbit.
What it really is: Welsh rarebit (the alternative spelling) is pretty much cheese on toast but with the welcome addition of beer, mustard and Worcestershire sauce. See, no rabbit at all.

Mincemeat
What you'd expect it to be: The same stuff you find in burgers and spaghetti bolognese.
What it really is: A sweet, spicy mixture of raisins, apples, spices and rum or brandy – i.e. the stuff you find in mince pies. But it wasn't always like this. In medieval times mincemeat was invented as a way to preserve actual meat, but as the years passed the meat content was reduced. These days you'll be hard pressed to find 'real' mincemeat anywhere.

Refried beans
What you'd expect it to be: Er, refried beans.
What it really is: Refried beans are not fried twice at all. In fact they're usually not even fried once. They are simply mushed-up pinto beans with seasoning. The word 'refried' comes from the Spanish word 'refrito' which means 'cooked well'.

Head cheese
What you'd expect it to be: A skull-dwelling pus-like discharge with a putrid smell.

(Continued)

What it really is: Head cheese is a type of sausage made with a boiled pig or calf head, typically without the brains, eyeballs or ears but with the tongue, feet and heart thrown in for flavour.

Sweetbreads
What you'd expect it to be: Delicious sugary bread, the sort of thing you might enjoy with afternoon tea.
What it really is: Sweetbreads are the paired thymus glands and pancreas of milk-fed calves. So not something you'd want with afternoon tea, then.

Hot dogs
What you'd expect it to be: A particularly warm canine.
What it really is: Well, you know, don't you? There definitely shouldn't be any dog in a hot dog these days, though there was at one time. In Germany, the home of the hot dog, the use of dog meat in sausages was fairly common until the twentieth century. Which is why the Germans nicknamed them 'dogs'.

Historians have long claimed that ice cream, or at least a precursor to what we know as ice cream, began some time during the Persian Empire (550–330 BC) when soldiers would pour grape juice and rosewater over snow and eat it as a refreshing treat. This Slush Puppy-like delicacy was particularly popular when the weather was hot – just as ice cream is today – and snow was saved in cool underground chambers known as yakhchal in order to make it. Indeed the lure of this flavoured ice was so strong that those without access to these prototype refrigerators would bravely ascend snow-capped mountains to get their icy sugary hit.

The Persians weren't the only ones at it. Civilizations have served iced foods for thousands of years. During the first century AD the Roman emperor Nero Claudius Caesar is said to have regularly sent his slaves high up into the Apennines to get snow to chill wines and fruit juices. The story goes that one day a careless slave spilled some saltpetre on this packed snow. Saltpetre speeds up the freezing process, so it turned the juices into slushy ice – a forerunner of what we now call sorbet. The Romans can't take all the credit, though. Some historians, particularly those in the Far East, believe it was the Chinese who first developed the technology for making ice, and with good reason: the adventurer Marco Polo returned to Europe from his thirteenth-century expeditions with recipes for delicious ices flavoured with exotic fruits and tales of their having been enjoyed in Asia for thousands of years. Some even say the Chinese were making ice cream from milk and spiced rice over four thousand years ago.

Wherever ice cream was first produced, there is little disagreement that it was Catherine de' Medici who made it popular in Europe. When the Italian duchess married the Duke of Orléans (Henry II of France) in 1533, her Italian chefs served a different flavour on each of the thirty-four days of the celebration. Their son, Henry III, became so addicted to the delectable treat that he demanded a generous daily dose. Not long after that Spanish physician Blasius Villafranca rediscovered the idea of using saltpetre to speed up the freezing process. His experiments led to the invention of the first home ice-cream freezer, consisting of little more than a set of metal bowls with salted ice packed between them. One hundred years later Charles I of England was, it is said, so impressed by this 'frozen snow' that he threatened his personal chef with beheading if he dared to share the palace's secret recipe. Unfortunately for Charles it was he who had his head lopped off, in 1649, which freed his chef to divulge everything.

Ice cream remained a privilege of the aristocracy right up until the publication of Mrs Mary Eale's *Receipts* in 1718 – a revolutionary English cookbook that for the first time revealed the recipe for ice cream to the common man. A dessert once reserved for royalty could now be made by anyone. Those who own a pail (bucket), some straw and some bay-salt (saltpetre) can have a go themselves: 'Take Tin

Ice-Pots, fill them with any Sort of Cream you like, either plain or sweeten'd, or Fruit in it; shut your Pots very close; to six Pots you must allow eighteen or twenty Pound of Ice, breaking the Ice very small; there will be some great Pieces, which lay at the Bottom and Top: You must have a Pail, and lay some Straw at the Bottom; then lay in your Ice, and put in amongst it a Pound of Bay-Salt; set in your Pots of Cream, and lay Ice and Salt between every Pot, that they may not touch; but the Ice must lie round them on every Side; lay a good deal of Ice on the Top, cover the Pail with Straw, set it in a Cellar where no Sun or Light comes, it will be froze in four Hours, but it may stand longer; then take it out just as you use it; hold it in your Hand and it will slip out. When you wou'd freeze any Sort of Fruit, either Cherries, Rasberries, Currants, or Strawberries, fill your Tin-Pots with the Fruit, but as hollow as you can; put to them Lemmonade, made with Spring-Water and Lemmon-Juice sweeten'd; put enough in the Pots to make the Fruit hang together, and put them in Ice as you do Cream.'

This recipe may sound a little rudimentary, but whether it's being made in your kitchen with a hand crank, at a local homemade ice cream shop with a mechanized ice cream maker, or in a factory that turns out thousands of tubs a day, the process of making ice cream is basically the same. The only difference is the scale of the operation. You take milk, sugar, cream and sometimes eggs, whip them all together, and freeze. Simple, right? Well, no, not really. While milk fat (sometimes also referred to as 'butterfat' or 'dairy fat') is the traditional source of fat for ice cream, due to a shortage of butter during (and for several years after) the Second World War UK manufacturers began making ice cream using vegetable oil. This continued even after food rationing ended, partly because vegetable oil is a lot less expensive than milk fat, but also because consumers had grown accustomed to it.

It remains standard practice for budget ice cream makers to use vegetable fat instead of milk fat, and a lot of supermarket ice cream is made this way. Legislation, which varies between countries, dictates whether or not these products can be labelled 'dairy ice cream' or 'ice cream'.

According to the Food Labelling Regulations (1996), all products sold as 'dairy ice cream' in the UK must contain at least 5 per cent fat and 2.5 per cent milk protein – that's all. Even more astonishingly, ice cream labelled simply 'ice cream' as opposed to 'dairy ice cream' can derive all of its 5 per cent fat from non-dairy sources. That's right: much of the ice cream we eat in the UK today is not required by law to include any cream whatsoever.

The three most common milk fat substitutes you'll find in your ice cream are coconut oil, palm oil and palm kernel oil. All three come with a number of benefits for the ice cream manufacturer: they're cheap (mainly because you don't need a cow to produce them), easy to transport and store (due to their long shelf life) and have fairly similar melting points to milk fat. However, while these fats are cheap and pretty good at mimicking milk, they don't come without their downsides.

Palm kernel oil and coconut oil contain a high level of saturated fatty acids, around 80 per cent and 90 per cent respectively, which means they are great for making ice cream but less impressive from a nutritionist's point of view. Palm oil has a lower saturated fat content (around 50 per cent) but a number of other drawbacks. First, it's pretty much solid at 35°C, which also happens to be the temperature of the human mouth. Thus some argue that ice cream made using palm oil often has an unpleasant waxy mouth-feel. More importantly, it is widely acknowledged that palm oil is produced at the expense of the environment. According to the Roundtable on Sustainable Palm Oil (RSPO), 99 per cent of all palm oil – found in a third of all products on supermarket shelves – is produced unsustainably. Indeed the vast majority of palm oil used in products like ice cream is sourced from countries such as Malaysia and Indonesia, where huge swathes of rainforest have been levelled in order to create vast monoculture palm oil plantations. The result, according to the World Wide Fund for Nature, is the destruction of critical habitat for large numbers of endangered species including rhinos, orang-utans, elephants and tigers. Fortunately, the environmental

The Five Most Bizarre Ice Cream Flavours of All Time

Think it's weird putting vegetable oil in ice cream? Take a look at these . . .

1. Human breast milk: In 2011 London ice cream shop The Icecreamists created a flavour of ice cream made using freshly expressed breast milk, blended with Madagascan vanilla pods and lemon zest. The ice cream was churned using donations from London mother Victoria Hiley then served with a rusk and an optional shot of Calpol or Bonjela.

2. Cheeseburger: At the Coromoto ice cream parlour in Venezuela you'll find over eight hundred flavoured ice creams, including cheeseburger – a blend of burger meat, cheese, French fries and various 'secret ingredients'. Customers say it's like having a Happy Meal and McFlurry all at once.

3. Coronation chicken: In 2012 Jacob Kenedy, chef and founder of Italian gelato emporium Gelupo in London, created a coronation chicken-flavoured ice cream for the Queen's Diamond Jubilee concocted from cumin, cayenne pepper, turmeric, Marsala-soaked sultanas and chicken jus.

4. Horse meat: The Japanese are an adventurous lot when it comes to eating, but this one takes the biscuit. In the Sunshine City shopping mall in Tokyo you'll find Ice Cream City, where you can sample an impressive array of flavours ranging from octopus to 'basashi vanilla', which features chunks of blended raw horseflesh.

5. Pizza: And finally, over to Max & Mina's Homemade Ice Cream and Ices in New York where the Becker brothers have created a pizza-flavoured ice cream made with a blend of fresh tomato, garlic and mozzarella.

threat is well publicised and has been widely acknowledged by producers and regulators, many of whom are attempting to curb the problem by researching new methods of sustainable palm oil production.

Finally, vegetable fats, unlike milk fats, are also largely colourless and tasteless, so the product requires the addition of a slew of unexpected extras. Annatto colouring, otherwise known as E160b, is often used to recreate the colour of clotted cream; emulsifiers such as diglycerides of fatty acids (E471) prevent the fat and water content separating into a greasy puddle; and stabilizers, often derived from gelatin or seaweed, are used to improve texture.

27

How do you smoke food without fire?

THE ADAGE TELLS US that where there is smoke there is fire. And where there is fire there has, for an extremely long time, been cooking. Thus it could be said that the act of smoking food is as old as the ancient craft of cookery itself. After all, it is near impossible to roast food over an open fire without infusing that food with the familiar barbecued flavour we all call 'smoky'.

Two hundred and fifty thousand years after man first tamed fire we humans have become rather proficient at the act of smoking. Indeed the technique is behind some of our most exquisite dishes. In Whitby herring are salted, splayed and then smoked over smouldering piles of sawdust in tar-laden Victorian chimneys (giving us kippers, as they are affectionately known); on the Isle of Man traditionally cured Manx bacon is left to wallow in oak smoke for a minimum of 168 hours; while master whisky makers in Scotland smoke their barley over decomposed grass, heather and moss, giving the world the genius that is peated Scotch whisky. These, of course, are just the tip of the iceberg; imagine a world devoid of such culinary delights as smoked salmon, paprika, lapsang souchong tea and, God forbid, pickle-laden pastrami sandwiches. Absolutely unimaginable.

Our primeval yearning for the flavour of smoke doesn't end there. Not content with traditionally smoked foods we humans have recently begun to apply the flavour of smoke to all manner of weird and wonderful foods including cheese, crisps, faux meat, nuts, chilli sauce and even baked beans – none of which have ever been anywhere close to a roaring open fire (other than in a cast-iron pot, in the latter's case). So how on earth are such foods made?

First, the real thing. Hunting for our Stone Age ancestors was undoubtedly a difficult, time-consuming and often perilous activity, which is why any excess meat was always preserved by hanging it out to dry. Fortuitously, the primitive dwellings of these hunter-gatherers (usually caves or basic huts) lacked chimneys, thus any hanging meat was quickly infused with smoke, and it wasn't long before humans realized that this kind of meat not only tasted more interesting than normal dried meat but also kept for longer. Over time this process was combined with pre-curing the food in salt or brine, resulting in a remarkably effective preservation process that was adapted by numerous cultures around the globe.

Smoke alone isn't sufficient for preserving food, it must be combined with other preservation methods, mainly because unless the meat or fish is sliced extremely thinly the smoke cannot penetrate throughout. Nevertheless smoke has a number of remarkable traits. With the help of salt, smoke can dry out food to such an extent that no bacterial life can survive. What's more, many of the phenol compounds found in wood smoke, like formaldehyde and acetic acid, are anti-microbial, which means they are particularly adept at slowing down bacterial growth. Finally, and importantly, smoking meat creates something called a 'smoke ring' – a region of pink-coloured flesh usually seen in the outermost 8 to 10 millimetres of smoked meats, formed when nitrogen dioxide from smoke mixes with water. For professional barbecue chefs in the southern states of America these smoke rings are a badge of honour, a sign that the cut of meat is smoked to perfection. But smoke rings are believed to have another function, too: they protect the meat's vulnerable outer layer from bacterial infection.

Some posit that the discovery of smoke as a form of preservation was perhaps one of the most important culinary breakthroughs in human history. Because as one of the very first forms of food preservation, well before the advent of refrigeration, it allowed primitive man to spend less time hunting and cooking and more time exploring, ruminating and bonding with fellow humans. Civilization as we know it was born. Smoking isn't all about preservation (or civilization), however. Today, it is the multitude of different flavours created by smoke that we prize most highly. As any food smoker worth his or her salt will tell you, the key to great flavour is the use of different varieties of wood – specifically hardwoods, which contain the holy trinity of cellulose, hemicelluloses and lignin.

Time for a bit of science. Cellulose and hemicelluloses are types of complex sugar molecules which, when burned effectively, caramelize and produce the rich honey-like colour we associate with well-smoked foods. These same molecules are also responsible for the trademark sweet, flowery and fruity aroma of smoked foods. Lignin on the other hand comprises phenolic molecules which produce a number of distinctive aroma compounds when burned, including the smoky, spicy, pungent guaiacol, phenol and syringol, and sweeter ones such as the vanilla-scented vanillin and clove-like isoeugenol. (Having trouble pronouncing any of these? You're not the only one.) Furthermore, hardwoods also contain small quantities of proteins which contribute to the delicious roasted flavours of some smoked foods.

The basic technique for smoking has barely changed since it was first stumbled upon thousands of years ago. There are two main ways to smoke food: hot and cold. In the former you suspend raw food over or very close to a crackling flame and let it cook – much like barbecuing. Cold smoking, on the other hand, maintains the food's temperature at about that of room temperature, so the food remains uncooked but takes on the flavour of the smoke. Whichever of the two techniques you choose to use you always start by brining the meat or fish, which removes any excess water. Then you dry it and stick it in a smoker. This can be anything from a do-it-yourself roasting tin stuffed with smouldering wood shavings (see page 196) to a giant commercial stainless-steel vat laden with specially selected wood chips.

How, then, are processed foods like crisps smoked? Surely not in a chimney? The answer is something known as liquid smoke, a type of flavouring often derided by smoked food purists but celebrated by the processed food industry. But what is this unusual ingredient? The answer, it turns out, is not as strange as it seems. As well as containing thousands of complex compounds, gases and oils, all smoke is jam-packed with water vapour. To extract this vapour, liquid smoke manufacturers construct large mounds of smouldering but not burning wood embers in huge steel vats. The smoke is trapped inside a chilled compression chamber. As the temperature of the hot smoke rapidly drops, a brown, smoky water vapour forms. This smoky water is then filtered to remove any impurities. It takes over 5kg of wood to create just 1kg of flavouring.

Unsurprisingly, not all liquid smokes are born equal. After the vapour is collected, good-quality liquid smoke manufacturers leave it to age, which has the effect of mellowing any unpleasant burnt-toast-like flavours while intensifying any desirable wood-like aromas. Really high-quality manufacturers will take it one step further and pipe the water straight from the compression tanks into airtight hardwood barrels made from aromatic woods like oak, hickory, mesquite and maple to deepen the flavour. The liquid can be kept like this for anything from two weeks to several years. Those at the lower end of the quality scale, however, are forced to make up for low-grade wood and short matur-ation times by including all manner of additional ingredients such as caramel for colour, molasses for sweetness and preservatives to extend shelf life. Whether high end or low end, the resulting liquid smoke is either sold to consumers in bottles or shipped in containers to large-scale food producers who load it into atomizers and spray it over foods such as bacon, hot dogs, jerky, tofu, cheese, marinades, sausages, chops, roasts and ribs.

Understandably, liquid smoke doesn't come without its critics.

Perhaps one of the biggest criticisms levelled at it is that it cuts corners at the expense of quality. The very reason so many people love and cherish traditionally smoked foods is the time-consuming processes used to make them. BBQ chefs in the Deep South of the US, for example, can spend a good two days tending to smouldering pits of ribs and beef brisket. For chefs like this, smoking is a valued way of life, an integral part of their region's cultural fabric.

So how can you tell if your favourite smoked food is the real deal or not? It's actually pretty simple. Any food that has been smoked will proudly boast the word 'smoked' on its label, whereas those foods made with liquid smoke will say 'smoke flavoured'.

How to Smoke Your Own Food

Smoking is one of the oldest forms of preserving meat and a great way to impart some fuggy, smoky flavour. The best thing about it? It's really easy to do, requiring little more than an old saucepan or BBQ.

First Things First

All meat and fish intended for smoking is best salted first. This has the effect of drawing out any excess water, thus helping to condense the smoky aroma. To do this, simply scatter a layer of table salt (no need for the expensive stuff) on a large plate or casserole dish then place the meat or fish on top and scatter on a further layer of salt. Leave for anything between ten minutes and an hour, depending on the size and thickness of the food. A small mackerel fillet, for example, usually requires no more than a quarter of an hour, but a whole salmon fillet or steak will probably take an hour. Next, give the meat or fish a good rinse, pat it dry, and you're good to go.

(Continued)

A Word on Smoking Times

The methods below are for cold smoking, which doesn't fully cook food but does impart a delicious smoky flavour. As with the salting, how long you smoke meat or fish for depends on its size and the depth of flavour you're after. But generally speaking it should take around two to three hours per kilo of protein. Remember, the meat or fish will still need to be cooked afterwards.

The Gas Stove Method

Things you'll need:
a large saucepan with a lid
a circular metal rack (like a cake rack), or some sturdy wire mesh
some untreated natural sawdust
a portable gas stove

First off, find a place to do this outdoors, preferably away from open windows. Scatter a layer of untreated food-grade sawdust across the bottom of the saucepan and suspend your rack or mesh a few inches above it. Now heat the saucepan on the stove. As soon as the sawdust begins to smoulder, place your salted meat or fish on the rack/mesh and put the lid on the saucepan.

The BBQ Method

If you already have a BBQ this is probably the easiest option. All you need to do is light a small fire and once it's settled down sweep the hot embers into the corners, away from the area where you intend to smoke your food. Then add a few handfuls of damp wood chips to the embers, which will encourage the production of more smoke. Finally place the food you intend to smoke on the grill, away from the embers. Close the lid and leave it. Simple as that.

(Continued)

What Wood?

Whatever your method, the key to great-tasting smoked food is picking the right kind of wood.

Oak: One of the most common woods used for smoking in the UK, and with good reason. It's incredibly versatile and works well with all kinds of fish and meat, particularly with more robustly flavoured meats like beef and lamb.

Hickory: The traditional wood used in Southern-style barbecues. An excellent choice for pork ribs, pulled pork or beef brisket. Hickory will impart a strong smoke flavour, so use in small amounts.

Mesquite: Famed for its extremely robust flavour. Best used with larger cuts of meat like beef brisket. Too much of this smoking wood will render your food inedible, so only use small amounts and mix it with other smoking wood until you get the balance just right.

Beech: Imparts a mild flavour that works well with both fish and meat. Often used as a neutral wood to help burn and dilute some of the stronger woods.

Apple: A medium-strength somewhat sweet smoking wood with a delicious fruity aroma. It's an excellent choice for chicken, pork ribs, pulled pork or bacon. And it can work well with cheese, too.

Alder: A light and slightly sweet smoking wood. It comes from the Pacific Northwest of America and has been traditionally used for fish. Works especially well with salmon.

Old barrels: When barrels for storing wine, whisky or chilli sauce are no longer useful for ageing they are often cut up and sold as smoking wood. The aromas produced by this wood can be really interesting – especially ex-bourbon barrels, which work amazingly well when cold-smoking Scottish salmon.

(Continued)

Birch: Particularly popular in Iceland and other northern European countries, where it is predominantly used to smoke fish.

28

Do detox diets work?

DOWNING LITRES OF CHILLI-INFUSED water, having gallons of coffee piped up your backside, being sucked by leeches and getting wrapped in clingfilm until your body overheats. No, not sadistic torture methods practised by Guantanamo Bay prison guards, just some of the 'detoxes' undertaken every year by millions in the pursuit of good health and beauty.

Of course, not all treatments are this bizarre. Visit your local spa or health food shop and you'll be sure to find all manner of pills, potions, creams, oils, smoothies, wraps and herbal teas that profess to cure a wide range of afflictions from tiredness to headaches, bloating to back pain, skin problems to constipation. According to their labels, they work by 'cleansing' and 'purifying' your body's blood and organs of a welter of accumulated 'toxic' chemicals.

And Brits, it seems, have swallowed these claims hook, line and sinker: over the past decade detoxing has grown from an obscure alternative quirk into a multi-million-pound industry endorsed by big-name celebrities like Oprah Winfrey, Gwyneth Paltrow and Cameron Diaz. Even Prince Charles has jumped on the bandwagon by marketing a Duchy Originals herbal 'detox tincture' featuring globe artichoke and dandelion. But what exactly are these detox products trying to flush out of our bodies, and do they really work?

If every New Year you find yourself perusing the shelves of health food shops in search of a miracle detox cure, then you are not alone. Sales of detox products increase massively every January as people scramble to undo some of the harm caused by festive over-indulgences. But toxins aren't just imbibed by us over the Christmas holidays, they are everywhere, all the time – in the food we eat, in the water we drink, even in the air we breathe. Indeed according to many experts our bodies are nearly always saturated with these toxic nasties.

Most of us are well aware of the dangers of too much caffeine, alcohol, sugar and salt, but there are other sinister substances in much of the food and drink we consume, such as mercury (found in species of fish like shark, swordfish, king mackerel, tuna, halibut and lobster), sodium nitrate (used to produce bacon, hot dogs, ham and sausages), bisphenol-A (a controversial industrial chemical used in food packaging and baby's bottles that has been linked to a range of human disorders including diabetes and obesity), and cadmium (an extremely toxic heavy metal found in some shellfish as well as the kidneys and livers of some livestock). Unfortunately, the list doesn't end there. Much of the food we eat contains hundreds more toxins including colourings, flavour enhancers, preservatives and pesticides; high-pesticide foods typically include non-organic peaches, strawberries, apples, nectarines, bell peppers, celery, cherries, lettuce and imported grapes and pears.

A number of toxins have also been found in water. According to Dr Robert D. Morris, a leading expert in the field of drinking water, US researchers found eighty-two different pharmaceutical compounds in lakes and rivers. These chemicals include chlorine, bleach, ammonia and the female sex hormone oestrogen, which scientists have shown is so potent it can alter the sex of freshwater fish. These chemicals inevitably find their way into water-treatment plants, which some argue are incapable of removing them. Whether these chemicals are present in drinking water at concentrations high enough to affect human health remains a subject of debate, but the risk is there.

And the onslaught doesn't end there. Most of us are well aware of the toxic properties of tobacco smoke, but even the simple act of breathing everyday air can cause an increase in our body's toxin levels. According to the Department for Environment, Food and Rural Affairs (Defra), every time we inhale oxygen we also inhale pollutants including nitrogen dioxide and sulphur dioxide, both of which irritate the airways of the lungs. In cities people are particularly prone to ingesting high amounts of carbon monoxide, a gas that prevents the uptake of oxygen by the blood, leading to a significant reduction in the supply of oxygen to the heart. According to one government report, pollutants like this could be causing over fifty thousand premature deaths a year.

Sounds absolutely terrible, doesn't it? The only solution, it seems, is to stay indoors, drink mineral water and eat organic vegetables. Well, perhaps not. Our bodies, it turns out, are remarkably efficient at processing toxins through organs like the liver and kidneys and through the digestive and lymphatic systems, which are designed to take out of our bodies anything unwanted and/or dangerous. The liver is highly adept at removing the toxins found in alcohol and some medications. As for the kidneys, these are one of the primary ways in which the body is able to eliminate toxic and waste products from the blood. They do this with the help of small structures called glomeruli which essentially work to filter undesirable substances out of the blood and concentrate them in urine, which is then excreted from the body via the bladder and urethra. Defecation performs a similar role. Another way in which our bodies can rid themselves of toxins is by sweating. Some toxic and waste products in the blood are able to diffuse into the sweat glands. As a result, when the body sweats (in order to cool down) some toxins are excreted in the process.

So if our internal detox systems do a pretty sterling job, what on earth is the point of coffee enemas, herbal tea and wheatgrass shots? Well, the basic idea behind a detox is that the modern world puts so much stress on our bodies and exposes us to such a large number of toxins on a daily basis that our natural mechanisms simply cannot keep up. As a result toxins hang around in our lymphatic and gastro-intestinal systems as well as in our skin and hair, causing problems such as tiredness, headaches and nausea. Temporarily give up the kinds of foods that top up these toxins and we'll give our bodies a chance to recover.

Helping the body to purge itself in this way isn't a new idea. Indeed colonic irrigation (where water is pumped into the colon through a tube inserted into the anus, to release faeces from the bowel wall) was invented by the Ancient Egyptians, who believed that excessive toxins in the intestines caused fever. And they weren't far off the mark: poor bowel regularity or a diet low in fibre can leave toxins stuck in the colon, and these will eventually be reabsorbed by the body. The Ancient Greeks practised detoxification too. They believed that an excess or deficiency of the body's four humours (blood, black bile, yellow bile and phlegm) caused an increase in toxins, resulting in poor health. In the Far East doctors have been practising detoxification for thousands of years. Practitioners of traditional Chinese medicine believe that the body sends toxins as far away from your heart as possible, which is why some of the most effective acupuncture points are believed to be in the lower legs and feet. Another traditional form of detoxification is cupping: cups made of strong glass are placed directly on to the skin at pressure points and suction is created with the use of a pump. Proponents of the practice say it stimulates blood circulation on acupressure points and helps to 'prevent stagnation', 'freeing up blockages'.

The idea of a detox diet, however, is a relatively new thing – a reaction to the increasing use of flavour enhancers, food colourings, pesticides and preservatives during the latter part of the twentieth century. Most of these regimes involve consuming extremely limited sets of foods (only water or juice, for example – a form of detoxing known as juice fasting), eliminating certain foods such as fats or processed foods, and avoiding suspected irritants. Other diets encourage people to consume high-fibre foods, which proponents claim cause the body to burn accumulated stored fats, releasing fat-stored 'toxins' into the blood which can then be excreted through the blood, skin, urine, faeces and breath.

But does detoxing actually work or is it a load of old quackery? Die-hard detoxers may want to look away now. Many of those within the medical establishment argue that detoxing is at best pointless, and at worst dangerous. The reason the idea of detoxification is flawed, say critics, is that even in today's toxic-rich environment the human body processes and removes harmful substances incredibly efficiently. The body's waste disposal system has had millions of years to evolve and works round the clock. The gut prevents bacteria and many other toxins from entering the body in the first place and our organs are constantly creating highly complex chemical reactions that turn food and drink into hormones and energy. Our metabolisms are also highly efficient at dissolving unwanted substances harmlessly into our urine and bile – a process that biologists call 'conjugation' – which enables us to get rid of them when we visit the toilet. Thus, critics argue, the idea of toxic chemicals simply sitting around in our bodies waiting to be purged by expensive detox regimes is nonsensical. Professor Edzard Ernst, for-merly professor of complementary medicine at the University of Exeter, argues that if detoxing really did work it would be simple to prove its effectiveness. 'All you would need to do is to take a few blood samples from volunteers and test whether this or that toxin is eliminated from the body faster than normal,' he says. 'But there are no studies that demonstrate this effectiveness. The reason is simple: these products have no real effects.'

Even abstaining from toxins won't do you any good, say experts. According to the British Liver Trust, giving up alcohol for one month is pointless, especially after the excesses of Christmas. Instead drinkers are far better off abstaining for a few days every week throughout the whole year. This is because the liver can repair itself very quickly, taking as little as twenty-four hours to get back to normal. If you abstain from alcohol for a month, therefore, you are doing yourself no extra favours; indeed you may be doing yourself some harm because it can lead to a false sense of security, feeding the idea that you can abuse your liver as much as you like through the year and then sort it out with a quick fix in January. While a lifetime of alcohol avoidance would be a solution, giving the stuff up for a month or so each year could even be harmful; some studies have found this to reduce the numbers of enzymes in your liver that help to process the toxins you put in – so when you next have a drink the effects might be even worse.

Detoxing can be actively bad for you in other ways, too, especially if you're young or suffer from any existing health conditions. Normal teenagers need lots of nutritional goodies like calories and protein to support rapid growth and development, so diets that involve fasting and severe restriction of food are never a good idea. Detox dieting has also been shown to be addictive because of the feelings of control that come with counting calories, potentially leading to eating disorders and other serious health problems. In 2008 a court awarded a woman £810,000 after a diet of six pints of water a day caused her irreparable brain damage. Within days of beginning the 'hydration diet' the woman was left fighting for her life after suffering hyponatraemia – the medical name for a water overdose – where a person's salt levels fall below an acceptable level.

It would, of course, be unfair to tarnish all forms of detoxing with the same brush. Or indeed to suggest there is no way to give your body a helping hand when it comes to removing toxins. One natural, effective and safe form of detoxing is exercise, which not only spurs the body's natural detoxifying organs into action (i.e. the lungs, metabolism and circulatory system) but also promotes sweating. Another safe and effective way to detox is to make sure you are fully hydrated. Sure, fresh fruit juices, herbal tea, kombucha tea and coconut water are ways to stay hydrated, but so is water. Just be sure not to overdo it.

The bottom line? The human body is designed to purify itself. But you can give it a helping hand by doing lots of exercise, staying hydrated and adopting a balanced, nutritious diet.

The Lowdown on Toxins

What are toxins? In the context of alternative medicine, toxins are accumulated chemicals or poisons believed to have harmful effects on the body.

Where do they come from? Humans are exposed to toxins from four main sources: food, water, air and chemicals. In food you find toxins in the form of additives, sulphites, dyes and chemical flavourings, while drinking water can contain toxins like chlorine, ammonia and even bleach. The main sources of toxins in air are methane, carbon dioxide and tobacco smoke. As for chemical toxins, these range from prescription and recreational drugs to unwashed non-organic fruit and vegetables, which often contain pesticides.

How does the human body get rid of them? Our bodies are very clever things. Healthy humans process toxins naturally with the help of organs like the liver and kidneys, which flush them out of our bodies in the form of sweat, urine and faeces. Our digestive, lymphatic and circulatory systems also play major roles in the removal of toxins.

If the body detoxes naturally, why do people detox? Because the idea has taken hold that our natural detoxification mechanisms cannot keep up in the modern world. 'Detoxing' refers to taking extra measures to ensure that your body removes harmful substances properly, to avoid any negative effects of toxin build-up.

Sounds convincing . . . what's the problem? Critics argue that many detox products make false claims that are scientifically unproven, while detox diets have been criticized for being addictive, harmful and ultimately useless.

(Continued)

Is there a safe way to detox? While the body does detox naturally, you can give it a helping hand by taking exercise (which encourages you to sweat), drinking lots of water (which will make you urinate more) and eating a balanced diet with high-fibre foods (to make your bowel movements more regular).

29

Are artificial sweeteners healthier than sugar?

YOU SEE THEM IN almost every eatery in Britain – those tiny pink, blue or yellow paper packets emblazoned Splenda, Canderel, Sweet'N Low or SucraPlus. In a little over a hundred years artificial sweeteners have gone from complete obscurity to an omnipresent part of the dining experience.

It is small wonder that where you once found a sugar bowl you're now much more likely to find a multicoloured collection of single-serving chemicals: Britain is currently in the grip of a well-publicized obesity crisis and our fear of calorific sugar is turning increasing numbers of us to artificial sweeteners in a desperate bid to beat the bulge. According to studies by market analysts Mintel, a total of 3,920 products containing artificial sweeteners were launched in the US between 2000 and 2005 alone including soft drinks, ready meals, cereals, chocolate bars, crisps, chewing gum, yoghurts, biscuits and fruit juices – many of which make big money on the UK market.

But there's a problem: in their 130-year history artificial sweeteners have gone from being a wonder drug to a cause célèbre blamed for all manner of horrific side effects including blindness, muscle spasms, shooting pains, seizures, headaches, depression, anxiety, memory loss, birth defects and cancer. But is this warranted? And what exactly are sweeteners anyway?

It is estimated that cardiovascular disease, diabetes and cancer kill 35 million people every year – and so far as the UN is concerned tobacco, alcohol and poor diet are the main culprits. But while governments have heavily regulated the first two in order to protect public health, poor diet continues with a free rein, causing more disease than smoking, alcohol and physical inactivity combined. The main cause of so many deaths? According to the experts, it's sugar, a food considered so unsafe by some it has been labelled 'the most dangerous drug of our time'.

It is with good reason that sugar now has a tarnished reputation: unlike fat and protein, refined sugars offer no nutritional value whatsoever and, contrary to what many of us believe, the body does not require any added carbohydrates from sugar for energy. Thus it is a source of completely useless and potentially deadly calories. Yet, scarily, sugars find their way into the majority of processed foods we eat. And, shockingly, guideline daily amounts for sugar have not been updated since 2004 when it was suggested each of us could consume a staggering 12 and a half teaspoons of the stuff daily (including sugars found naturally in fruits, vegetables and milk products etc.). To put that into perspective, the Scientific Advisory Commission on Nutrition (SACN) has recently been advised by scientific experts that added sugar should constitute no more than 5 per cent of energy: that would give a limit to the average man of eight teaspoons a day and the average woman six teaspoons. Yet one regular-sized chocolate bar alone is likely to contain eight teaspoons of sugar, which is almost triple the maximum amount recommended for four- to eight-year-olds by the US Department of Health.

With so many of us overdoing it on sugar, Type 2 diabetes – an entirely preventable disease – is on the increase, leading to a rise in the incidences of heart attacks, strokes, kidney failure, eye disease and leg amputations. The cost of diabetes to the UK is estimated to be over £24 billion a year, and projected to be more like £40 billion by 2030. If we do nothing, this could cripple the National Health Service. It is statistics such as these that have led to the growing popularity of artificial sweeteners – food additives that duplicate the taste of sugar, usually with the added benefit of being far sweeter and with fewer calories. Great news if you're on a diet.

The majority of sweeteners approved for food use are created synthetically in laboratories but contrary to popular belief some are also created entirely naturally with the help of plants. One of the most popular of these is a sugar substitute derived from *Stevia rebaudiana*, a species of plant native to South America and Mexico, where its leaves have been used as both a medicine and tea sweetener for at least 1,500 years. *Stevia*'s sweetness is all down to a compound known as steviol glycoside found in the plant's leaves. Manufacturers of *Stevia*-derived sweeteners extract the compound by placing the dried leaves of the plant into hot water and then reducing and filtering the infused liquid until it's 95 per cent steviol glycoside. The resulting pure white crystalline powder contains approximately the same number of calories as sugar but is around three hundred times sweeter.

Not all sweeteners are derived from nature, though. Indeed the vast majority of sweeteners we consume, such as saccharin, sucralose, neotame, cyclamate and aspartame (or E951 as it's called on food packaging), are created in laboratories. It is these sweeteners that have garnered the most negative press. The spectre of carcinogens first surfaced in the late 1960s when a series of studies appeared to prove a link between artificial sweeteners and cancer. In 1969 the sweetener sodium cyclamate was banned in the US after a study found that rats fed the equivalent of 250 cans of diet drink a day developed bladder tumours. In the 1970s saccharin was also discovered in one study to raise the risk of bladder cancer in rats. Then in 2005 scientists at the Ramazzini Foundation in Bologna, Italy, published research claiming that aspartame caused several types of cancer in rats at doses very close to the current acceptable daily intake for humans. However the European Food Safety Authority (EFSA) assessed the study and raised a number of concerns regarding it – suggesting the study was flawed.

Finally, in 2010 an EU-funded project found that pregnant women who consume fizzy drinks containing artificial sweeteners appear to be at greater risk of having a premature baby. The researchers from the Statens Serum Institut in Copenhagen looked at nearly sixty thousand Danish women who reported on their diet, including how many soft drinks they had each day, at around twenty-five weeks into their pregnancy. Around 5 per cent of women delivered their babies before thirty-seven weeks (full term). Women who had at least one serving of artificially sweetened soda a day while they were pregnant were 38 per cent more likely to deliver prematurely than women who drank no diet soda at all. Women who had at least four diet sodas a day were a shocking 80 per cent more likely to deliver prematurely.

All of these studies, however, should be taken with a massive pinch of salt, say the authorities who remain adamant that there is no conclusive proof of the relationship between sweeteners and ill health and argue that many of the studies that supposedly prove the link were fundamentally flawed. Cyclamate, saccharin and aspartame, for example, have since been deemed safe in Europe and fifty countries worldwide. In addition, not all of the chemicals found in artificial sweeteners are as unnatural as we may think. For example, as the body breaks down aspartame three chemicals are produced: phenylalanine, aspartic acid and methanol. It is these breakdown products that have been blamed for many of the sweetener's health scares. Yet both phenylalanine and aspartic acid occur naturally in proteins like fish, meat, eggs, avocados and asparagus. Methanol occurs naturally too – in fruit juice, for instance. Indeed a single serving of skimmed milk provides around six to nine times more phenylalanine and thirteen times more aspartic acid than the same amount of beverage sweetened with aspartame; a serving of tomato juice provides about four to six times more methanol than the same amount of an aspartame-sweetened beverage. Ultimately it doesn't matter what the source of these chemicals is as your body will deal with them in exactly the same way.

It should also be pointed out that artificial sweeteners are rigorously tested, probably more so than any other food ingredient. Aspartame, for

Artificial Sweeteners: Myths Debunked

Artificial sweeteners have skyrocketed in popularity over the past few decades. But are they all they're cracked up to be?

1. If biscuits are made with artificial sweeteners I can eat more of them.

False. While it's well known that large quantities of sugar are not good for us it is important to remember that sugar is only one calorific component of baked goods. Oils, flours, nuts and other ingredients can soon add up too. What's more, when sugar is removed, saturated fats are often added to make up for it, and according to the NHS, eating a diet high in saturated fat can raise the level of cholesterol in the blood, increasing the risk of heart disease.

2. It is proven that artificial sweeteners cause cancer.

False. Questions about artificial sweeteners and cancer arose when early studies showed that cyclamate and saccharin caused bladder cancer in rats. However, results from subsequent carcinogenicity studies of these sweeteners have not provided clear evidence of an association with cancer in humans. This position is supported by multiple regulatory agencies like the FSA as well as charities like Cancer Research, which says that 'large studies looking at actual people have now provided strong evidence that artificial sweeteners are safe for humans'.

3. Artificial sweeteners can help you to lose weight.

True. Artificial sweeteners can be anywhere from thirty to eight thousand times sweeter than sugar, which means that artificially sweetened foods generally contain far fewer calories than those made with sugar. This can be useful for those looking to lose weight because it enables them to eat sweet foods while sticking to a low-calorie diet.

example, has been approved for use in the UK since 1982 and during this time it has been subjected to over five hundred studies looking for any potential adverse effects. According to the Food Standards Agency (FSA), 'The weight of existing evidence is that aspartame is safe at current levels of consumption as an artificial sweetener. There is no evidence to suggest a need to revise the outcome of the earlier risk assessment or the Acceptable Daily Intake (ADI) previously established for aspartame of 40 milligrams per kilogram of body weight per day.' In the real world this means you would have to drink fourteen cans of artificially sweetened fizzy pop to exceed your ADI. And this daily limit is actually set at a hundred times less than the smallest amount that might cause health concerns. When you compare this to sugar, the relatively low risk of sweeteners becomes startlingly apparent. An average British adult is recommended not to exceed 50g of added sugar per day. A can of sugary drink contains around 40g of sugar – just two cans and you have exceeded your daily allowance. The safety of artificial sweeteners is even backed up by prominent organizations like Cancer Research UK, who state, 'Artificial sweeteners are used in a wide variety of foods and drinks. Almost everyone in developed countries consumes them, whether they know it or not. Because of this, any potential cancer risks would be very far-reaching. But overall, studies on artificial sweeteners have found that they do not increase the risk of cancer.'

30

Will 'lite' foods help you to lose weight?

B E IT THE ATKINS, Dukan or Beverly Hills, every year hundreds of
thousands of people across Britain embark on diets in a valiant
effort to beat the bulge. Indeed so convinced are we by the merits of
controlling what we eat it is estimated that the average forty-five-year-
old Brit has been on sixty-one diets. As a result the diet industry is
booming, weighing in at a colossal £2 billion – much of it amassed by
the manufacturers of 'lite', 'low fat' processed foods that are supposed to
help us get slimmer.

Yet with consumption of diet foods at an all-time high, Britain is at
the same time in the grip of a never-before-seen obesity crisis; 60 per
cent of the population are overweight, which costs the NHS an estimated £5 billion a year. Shockingly, on average we are all three stones
heavier than we were in the 1960s. In 1966 the proportion of people
with a BMI of over 30 (classified as obese) was a lithe 1.2 per cent
for men and 1.8 per cent for women; by 1989 these figures had bloated
to a whopping 10.6 per cent for men and 14 per cent for women.
Unfortunately these increases show no signs of abating.

But if we are consuming more 'lite' diet foods than ever before, why
are we the fattest we've ever been? Contrary to popular belief we are no
greedier than we were fifty years ago (though admittedly there are
no studies that prove this) and according to most statistics we are no

less physically active. Indeed levels of gym membership and sports participation have never been higher, while according to a twelve-year study conducted by Plymouth Hospital, children's physical activity has remained at the same level.

It is widely accepted that the main cause of obesity in the UK is the spread of fast food outlets and the growing consumption of cheap, unhealthy food and drinks. Take a stroll down almost any high street at half three in the afternoon and the chances are you'll find at least one fast food restaurant brimming with school-aged adolescents stocking up on chicken and chips (and for most, that's pre-dinner). Visit your local supermarket and you'll find shelf upon shelf of fatty, calorific processed foods. It is no secret these are the things that are making us plump. Indeed the dangers have been widely publicized by chefs such as Gordon Ramsay, Jamie Oliver, Heston Blumenthal, Marco Pierre White and many others whose TV shows and cookbooks encourage us to eat more healthily.

Undoubtedly some of this publicity has led to real change. Jamie Oliver's efforts to improve school meals, chronicled in the TV series *Jamie's School Dinners*, challenged the junk-food culture by showing schools they could serve healthy, cost-effective meals that kids enjoyed eating. As a result the government invested an extra £280 million in the school meals plan, limited the frequency of fried food sold at schools to twice-weekly and banned the sale of soft drinks to pupils. In a bid to encourage more health-conscious punters, fast food restaurant chains like McDonald's and Burger King have been impelled to introduce new 'low fat', 'lite' options.

Food manufacturers, however, cleverly caught on to the trend for diet foods long before fast food restaurants did. When rising levels of obesity were first spotted in the 1970s some of the world's biggest food conglomerates decided they should buy into the diet industry. Weight Watchers, a brand created by New York housewife Jean Nidetch in the early 1960s, was bought by Heinz in 1978, which in turn sold the company in 1999. In 2000 Slimfast, a liquid meal replacement invented by chemist and entrepreneur Danny Abraham, was bought by Unilever, which also owns Ben & Jerry ice cream and Wall's sausages. Then in 2011 the US weight loss brand Jenny Craig was bought by Swiss multinational Nestlé, which also sells copious amounts of chocolate and ice cream.

So with some of the largest food producers in the world making money from our insatiable appetite for dieting, it is no wonder processed 'lite' food can be found everywhere.

How exactly do these companies make processed foods 'lite' or 'low fat'? Well, it's all a matter of percentages. The Food Standards Agency says that to be able to make this claim the product in question must be at least 30 per cent lower in at least one typical value (listed on the label on the back of the pack), such as calories or fat, than standard products. Amazingly, one of the most common ways to do this is simply to make the product 30 per cent smaller. To put that into perspective, that would be the equivalent of ordering a deep-fried chicken burger at your local takeaway and punching a hole through its middle, leaving it looking a bit like a meaty polo mint. Weight for weight this product may contain more calories, saturated fat and salt than a regular chicken burger but it can still be sold as a diet-friendly 'lite' food.

Are consumers really that gullible? Well, the next step for the food manufacturer is to exploit our perception of what healthy food is. To return to the idea of a polo-mint-shaped chicken burger: all that would be necessary would be rebranding it in such a way that it exuded health, wholesomeness and, most importantly, weight loss. This could, perhaps, be done by calling it the 'Chicken-lite Bagel Burger' (because bagels have an association with healthiness). Then the only thing left would be to wrap the burger in green packaging (because as we all know people associate the colour green with goodness) with superimposed photos of fruit, vegetables and weighing scales and adorn it with wording such as '30 per cent less fat' and 'a natural source of protein and vitamin B6' – both of which are completely honest claims that reinforce the image of the product as a low-fat wholesome food. The moral of the story: never judge a food by its cover, no matter how green it is.

In 2003 an investigation by the Consumers' Association (CA) criticized a number of foods branded as 'lite' as being highly misleading. Indeed the investigation found that some foods labelled as such had seven times more fat than those described as 'low fat', which by law have to have no more than 3 per cent fat. Among the misleading products was a 'light' cream cheese, which was found to contain a massive 16 per cent fat. 'It is incredible that food manufacturers can get away with using terms like "lite" and "light" which to most shoppers will mean "low fat",' said a spokesperson from the association.

As well as the 'lite/light' loophole, the CA investigation found other ways in which diet foods dupe health-conscious consumers into buying them. One such way was for brands to make foods sound like they are low fat by the clever use of wording. A Soreen Snack fruit loaf, for example, claimed to be '90 per cent fat free', which in reality means it contains 10 per cent fat – which in terms of health is actually very high. In the same investigation manufacturers were accused of making false claims in a product's name or slogan. Rowntree's Fruitsome cereal bars (no longer available) were found to carry the slogan 'Good food, good life' despite the bars containing a tooth-aching 38 per cent sugar. Meanwhile, Walkers Lite crisps were advertised as 33 per cent less fat but still contained 22 per cent fat. These products were not breaking the law in any way, and the brands in question may well argue that their labels were both easy to understand and devoid of any phony claims. Nonetheless, the Consumers' Association said they were giving a false impression to consumers.

Not all diet foods are guilty of duping consumers. Some are very low in both fat and sugar. But that's not to say they are necessarily healthy. It is widely acknowledged that when you remove the natural fats and calories in food you have to make up for it otherwise the food will just taste bland. For some processed diet food manufacturers the answer is to incorporate additives, flavourings, preservatives and colourings in order to make the food resemble the real thing. Diet dairy spreads, for example, aimed at the health-conscious market, often do have less saturated fat than normal butter but instead of fat sometimes contain increased levels of salt.

Low-calorie food ought to be filling (a quality known to be inherent in many whole foods) otherwise people are likely to replace the calories later. So Britain's dieters, take note: lite isn't always right.

Diets Through History: The Good, the Bad and the Scary

From Lord Byron's potatoes and vinegar to the Victorian craze for swallowing tapeworms, the search for the elixir of weight loss has been going on for centuries.

Potatoes and vinegar: Lord Byron was one of the first diet icons and helped kick off the public's obsession with how celebrities lose weight, says historian Louise Foxcroft. In 1806 Byron weighed 13st 12lb (88kg). His horror of being 'fat' led him to take up a shockingly strict diet, partly to get thin and partly to keep his mind sharp. Existing solely on biscuits and soda water or potatoes drenched in vinegar, by 1811 the poet managed to get his weight down to under 9st (57kg) – a huge weight loss of nearly 5st (32kg).

Rubber: In the mid-1800s Charles Goodyear figured out how to improve the natural state of rubber with a process called vulcanization. Strangely, this prompted clothing manufacturers to start making rubber knickers and corsets. The thinking behind both was that rubber held in fat but more importantly made the wearer sweat, hopefully leading to weight loss. Unfortunately the constant presence of sweat made users vulnerable to all kinds of unspeakable infections.

The chewing craze: At the turn of the twentieth century American entrepreneur Horace Fletcher decided a lot of chewing and spitting was the key to weight loss. Fletcherism, as it became known, promoted chewing a mouthful of food

(Continued)

until all 'goodness' was extracted, then spitting out the fibrous material that was left. Not only were the bowel movements of those who followed Fletcherism few and far between, they were said to be completely odourless.

Tapeworms: During the Victorian era dieters would swallow beef tapeworm cysts, usually in the form of a pill. The theory was that the worms would grow inside the intestines and absorb food. It was a risky diet: tapeworms can grow up to 30ft in length, causing headaches, eye problems, meningitis, epilepsy and dementia. Worse still, at some point they have to be excreted.

Cigarettes: In 1928 cigarette brand Lucky Strike launched their 'For a Slender Figure Reach for a Lucky instead of a Sweet' campaign. Amazingly, it worked. The brand became synonymous with slimming, which helped to raise the company's market share by more than 200 per cent, making it the most profitable cigarette brand for two years running. Partly as a result of the campaign cigarettes continue to be associated with weight loss.

Cabbage soup: A radical weight-loss diet that involves consuming almost nothing but cabbage soup for seven days straight. Some cabbage-soup dieters claim to have lost around 5kg in just a week. However, scientists point out that most of this is water and not fat, and therefore not permanent. In addition the number of calories consumed per day while on the diet is considered unsafe.

Index

Daniel Tapper is an award-winning editor and full-time food writer. As staff writer for *Waitrose Kitchen,* Daniel wrote the popular feature *The Intrepid Foodie,* which examined the provenance, social significance and modes of manufacture of individual ingredients and food products. In 2010, Daniel founded and edited an award-winning magazine, *Bread and Butter,* dedicated to artisanal British food and drink. He is the co-founder of Something About Food. Daniel has contributed to the *Guardian* and other publications on issues associated with food, farming, brewing and dining.